AF428750

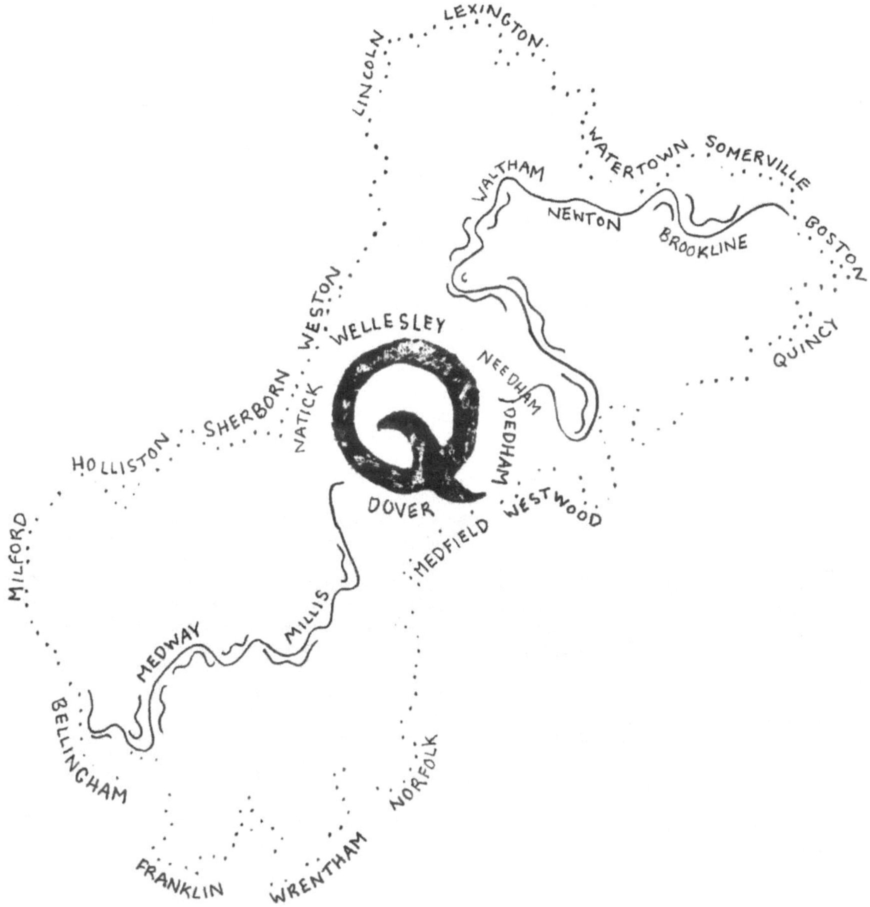

LEXINGTON
LINCOLN
WATERTOWN
SOMERVILLE
WALTHAM
NEWTON
BROOKLINE
BOSTON
WESTON
WELLESLEY
SHERBORN
NATICK
NEEDHAM
QUINCY
HOLLISTON
Q
DEDHAM
DOVER
WESTWOOD
MILFORD
MEDFIELD
MEDWAY
MILLIS
BELLINGHAM
NORFOLK
FRANKLIN
WRENTHAM

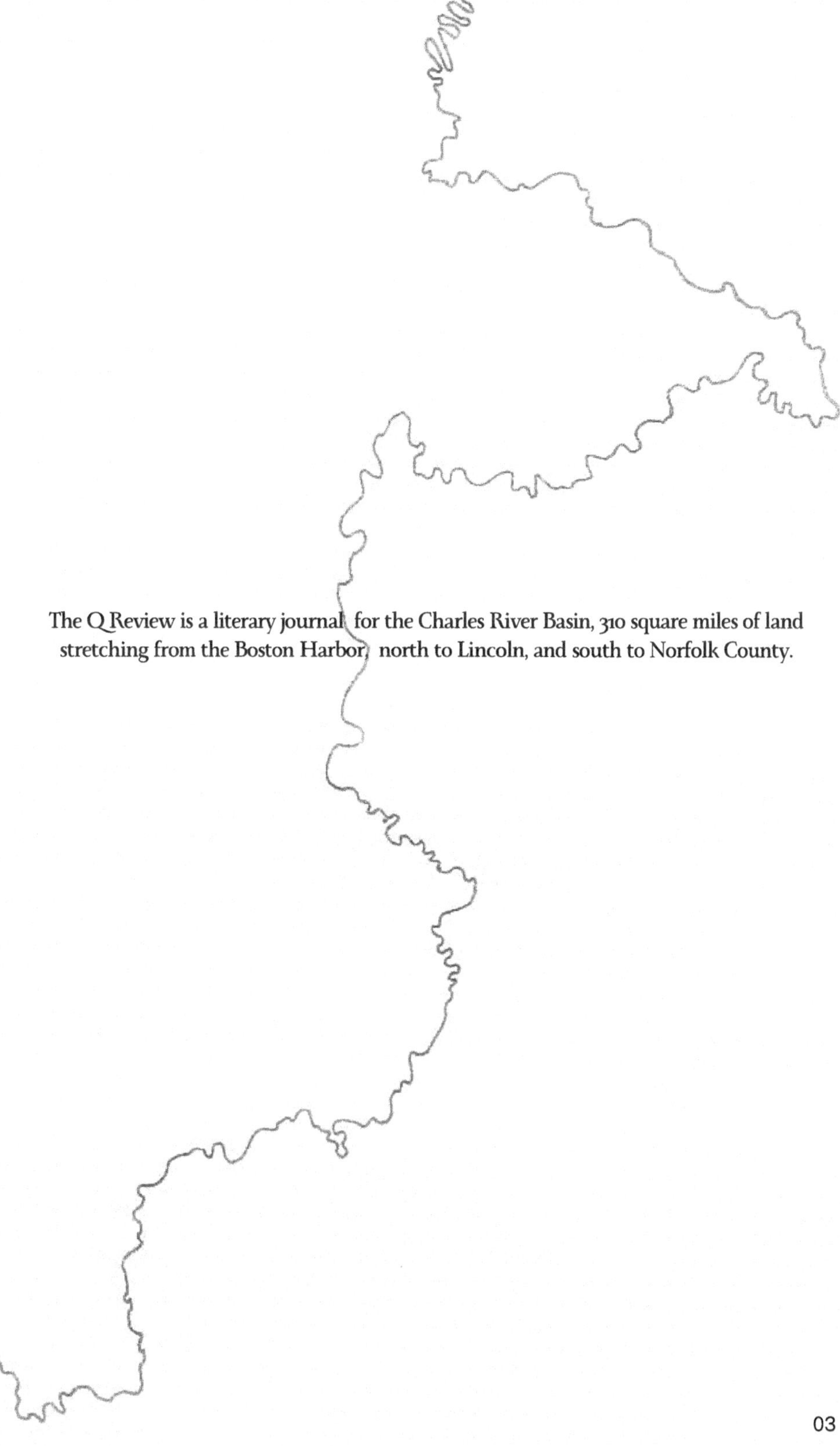

The Q Review is a literary journal for the Charles River Basin, 310 square miles of land stretching from the Boston Harbor, north to Lincoln, and south to Norfolk County.

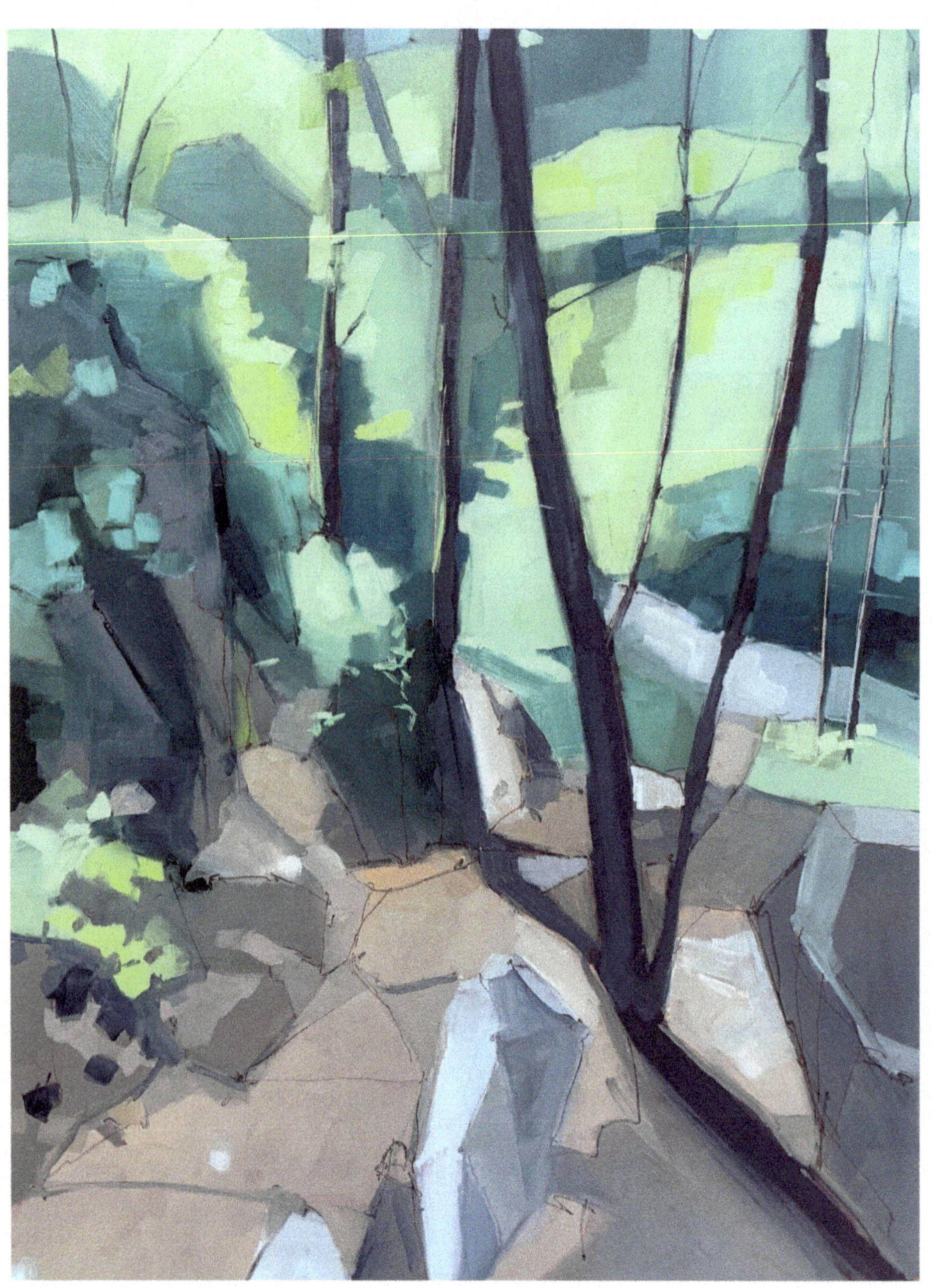

FOREST BATHING — JOHN RUFO

LETTER FROM THE EDITOR

It is summer in the watershed! Season of double-parked U-Hauls and mattresses blocking the sidewalks; of blinding commutes east and the sense of possibility at the end of the work day; of berry picking and park sprinklers; of backyard barbecues and string lights on porches and party sounds floating on warm evening air. This is a season for being together, and these are your own words (11).

In June, we hosted our first Neighborhood Salon at Newtonville Books, inspired by the tradition of 18th century salons, where great thinkers would convene at someone's home to discuss a specific topic over food and drinks. The Q is about being where your feet are, so it felt right to gather in person. Our guests were our neighbors, and our topic was "home."

Learning about where we live can be incredibly connecting and grounding. It is a call back to the physical in a world that is always online. It is a way to preserve local culture in an era of rapid globalization. It makes us better stewards for a landscape that needs us more than ever. And it is truly world expanding; it reminds us that the same place can mean so many things to so many people.

At the Salon, we heard from prior contributors on what this place means to each of them. We also answered questions about home: *What does it mean to (really!) know a place? What is something you want to know about your neighborhood?* One guest wanted to know, "What magic features have I become blind to?"

This issue investigates what is hiding in plain sight. Urban trail builder Miles Howard stitches together a 27-mile adventure of Boston's greenest and most walkable pathways (15). Erwin Kamuene unearths both the deep claustrophobia and wide open possibility of living in Boston (21). "Streetscape Curator" Matthew Dickey surfaces lesser-known histories from architectural clues (35).

This journal itself is an act of curation, a sliver of summer in the watershed through many different perspectives. I hope it helps you find the magic hiding right outside your door. Whether you find your way in by boat (30), by bike (35), or by foot (15); through an overgrown meadow in Westwood (12) or a pizza parlor in Hyde Park (26), we are so happy that you're here.

POETRY

IT WAS TOO WET.......................12
LINDA N. CABOT

WITHOUT EDGES....................22
JOHN RUFO

PROSE

RUNAWAY BRIDE 21
ERWIN KAMUENE

**A NEW PERSPECTIVE
ON THE HARBOR**....................30
ABBEY CAHILL

INTERVIEW

WALKING CITY TOUR 15
MILES HOWARD

ART

NEIGHBORHOOD PORTRAITS......25
TAHIRA MUHAMMAD & SAM LINBERG

STREETSCAPE CURATOR...........34
MATTHEW DICKEY

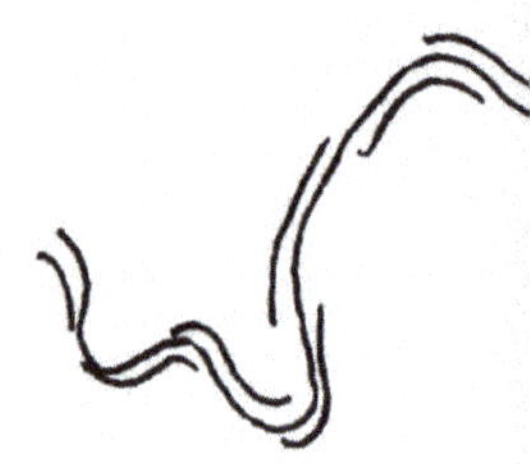

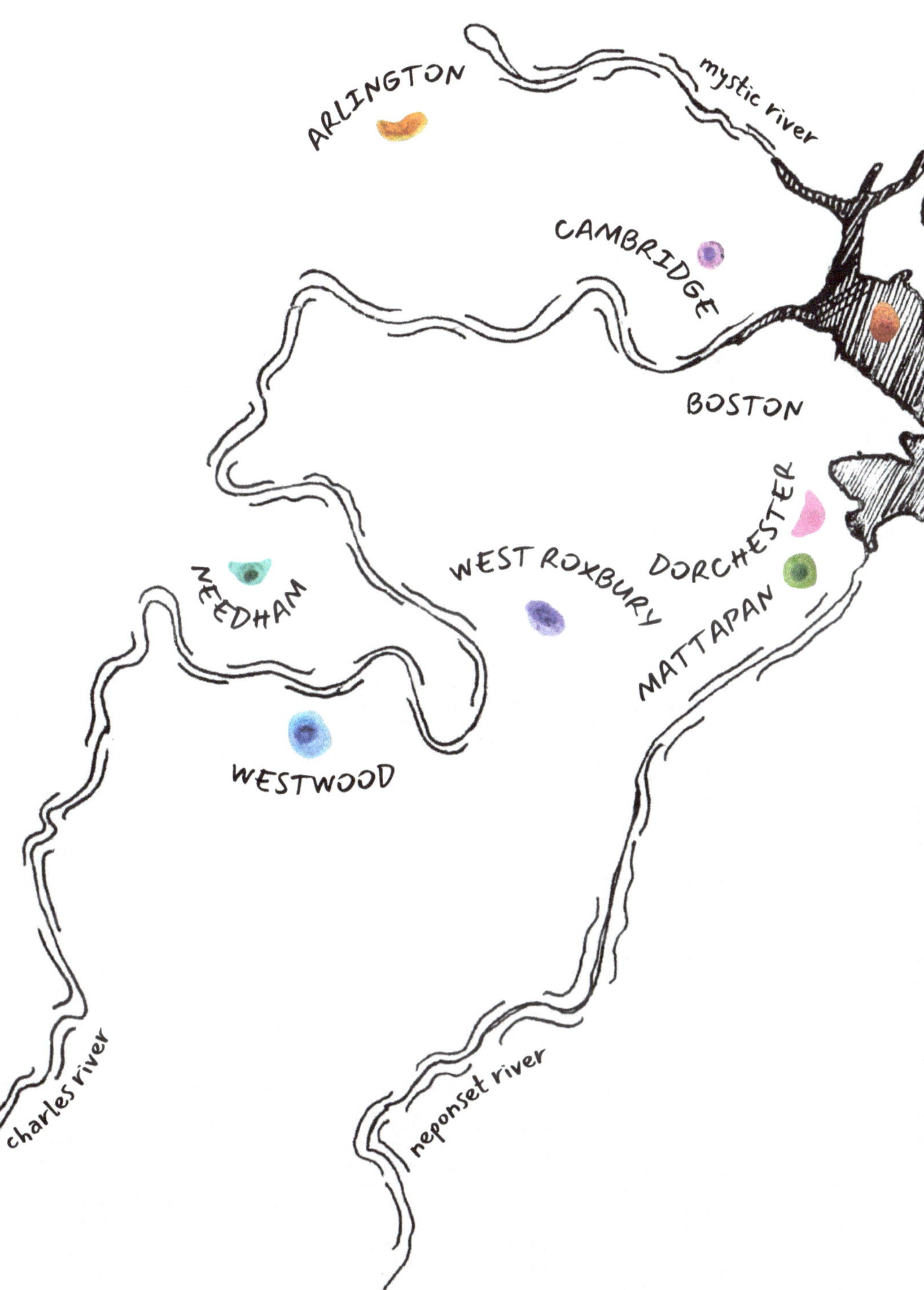

ARLINGTON
mystic river
CAMBRIDGE
BOSTON
DORCHESTER
WEST ROXBURY
MATTAPAN
NEEDHAM
WESTWOOD
charles river
neponset river

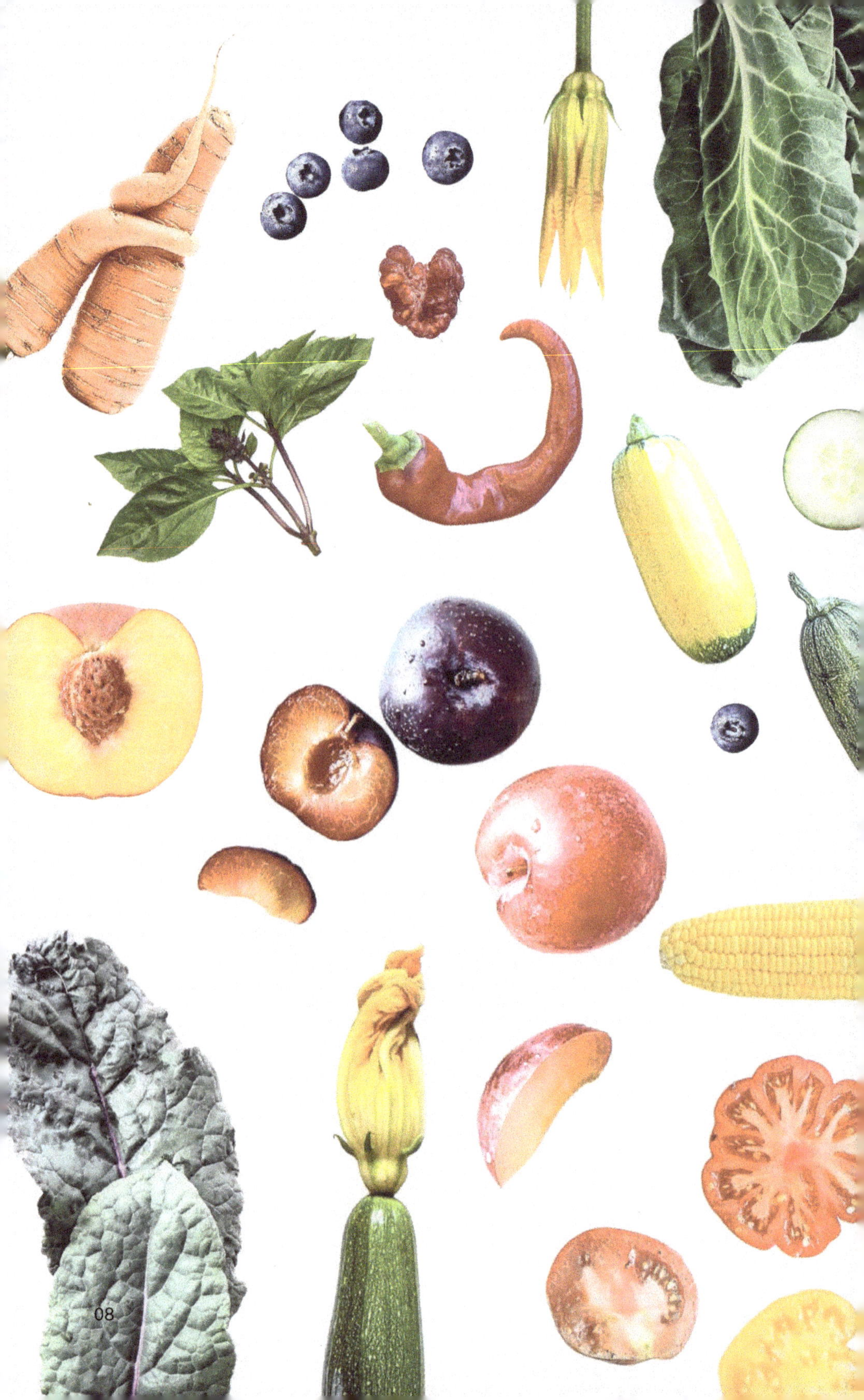

SUMMER FARMERS MARKETS

ARLINGTON	29 MYSTIC ST	WEDS 2 - 6:30
BRIGHTON	30 CHESTNUT HILL AVE	WEDS 2 - 6:30
BELMONT	10 CLAFLIN ST	THURS 2 - 6:30
CAMBRIDGEPORT: "CHARLES RIVER"	THE MORSE SCHOOL	SAT 10 - 2
CHARLESTOWN	MAIN ST & AUSTIN ST	WEDS 2 - 6
CHINATOWN	AUNTIE KAY & UNCLE FRANK CHIN PARK	SAT 10 - 2
COPLEY SQUARE	227 DARTMOUTH ST	TUES & FRI 11 - 6
DAVIS SQUARE	44 DAY ST	WEDS 12 - 6
DEDHAM	670 HIGH ST	WEDS 2 - 6
FENWAY: "CHARLESGATE"	461 COMMONWEALTH AVE	SUN 11 - 2
FRANKLIN	200 MAIN ST	FRI 2 - 6
FRAMINGHAM	2 OAK ST	THURS 3 - 7
JP CENTRE	677 CENTRE ST	SAT 12 - 3
LINCOLN	145 LINCOLN ROAD	SAT 9 - 1
MEDFIELD	29 NORTH ST	SUN 9 - 1
MILLIS	142 EXCHANGE ST	WEDS 2 - 6
NATICK	NATICK COMMON	SAT 9 - 2
NEWTON (TUESDAY)	1094 BEACON ST	TUES 1:30 - 6
NEWTON (SATURDAY)	352 LOWELL AVE	SAT 9:30 - 12:30
NUBIAN SQUARE	2300 WASHINGTON ST	SAT 11 - 3
ROSLINDALE	4225 WASHINGTON ST	SAT 9 - 1:30
UNION SQUARE	66 UNION SQUARE	SAT 9 - 1
WALTHAM	65 LEXINGTON ST	SAT 9:30 - 2
WATERTOWN	149 MAIN ST	WEDS 2:30 - 6:30

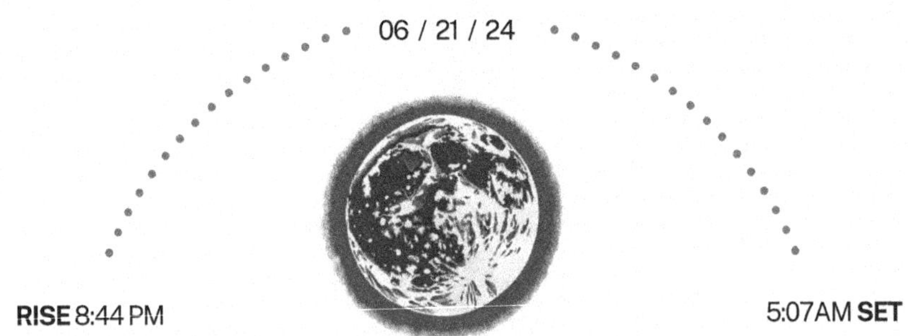

JUNE, STRAWBERRY MOON: STRAWBERRIES RIPEN; TIME TO PICK!

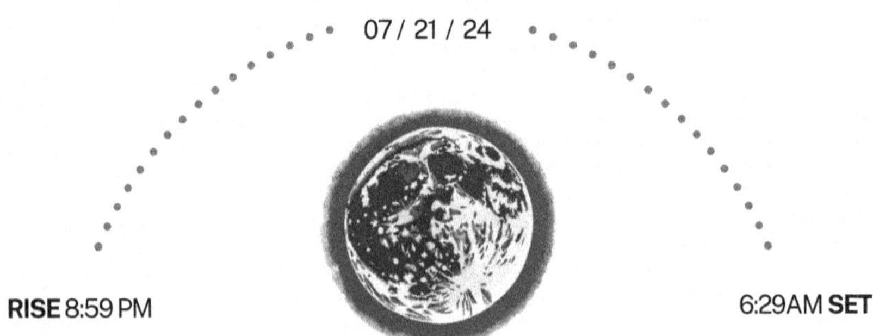

JULY, BUCK MOON: MALE DEER (BUCKS) HAVE LARGE ANTLERS AT THIS TIME OF YEAR. THEY SHED AND REGROW THEM ANNUALLY.

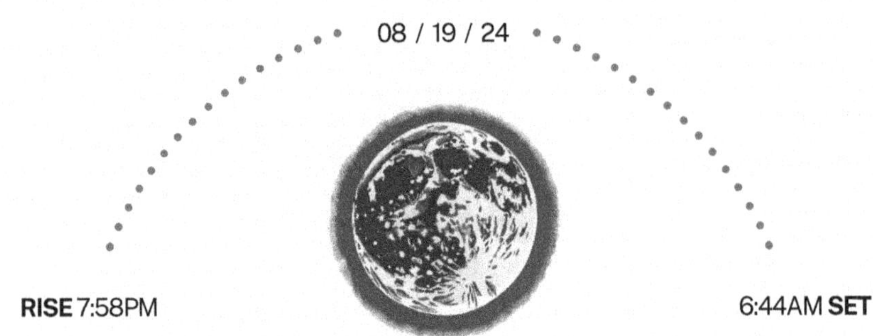

AUGUST, CORN MOON: FARMS THROUGHOUT THE CHARLES RIVER WATERSHED BEGIN HARVESTING CORN.

SOURCE: OLD FARMER'S ALMANAC. INDIGENOUS CULTURES HAVE LONG USED THE MOON TO TRACK SEASONAL HAPPENINGS (EXAMPLES: "13 MOONS, A HISTORY OF WAMPANOAG CULTURE," RECORDED BY CARY MEMORIAL LIBRARY, SEPTEMBER 2022; MASHANTUCKET PEQUOT MUSEUM, KUNÂHNEEPAMUHSHÂTUNÔNAK "OUR MOONS" EXHIBIT

- Blinding Commutes East
- The Sense of possibility after the work day
- Confused commercial HVAC Systems that leave spaces feeling damp - like a terrarium

In the community garden plot near Walden Pond that I tend to, last year's 2 strawberry starts have become 12 effusive plants. The birds can't believe it's already strawberry season, and all but 3 rabbit bitten red ones have been niv

U-Hauls Everywhere

① My daily dog walk happens earlier — or later — to keep my hair-covered companion from overheating on her favorite part of the day, a walk around the mystic river.

② soft serve at momma's grocery in cambridge

Signs of summer, yes, the slick of pollen. Mattresses blocking the sidewalk and turning grey-brown with rain + dirt. Graduation dresses, party sounds floating on warm evening air, my kids coming home wet from the sprinklers at the park.

- I have to push forward the timer on the porch string lights.

Hearing my dad mow the lawn at 5am.

It Was Too Wet
Linda N. Cabot

It was too wet to mow
the island fields
so, they glowed like
summer tourists and fireflies.

This afternoon I off-roaded,
driving our hybrid through
the tall blooming grass -
it tickled the undercarriage
with a sweeping, brushing strum.

The fields are brimming,
they burst like fireworks
and song with unabandoned
glee.

The scented milkweed
yellow trefoil and purple vetch -
together blooms
embracing the bee's roam
and flurry like sugary honey.

I wish to be a giant,
to kickback and lay lazy,
stretching over these
soft bedding fields, and
watch the wandering clouds
loll by.

My quilt of bent grass, soft rush,
and woodland sage -
begs me to sleep into the musky
woody smell of soft meadow -

And dream like Gulliver and voyage
into the wild knowing of these flowing
forever fields –

Now free from human touch –
I can disappear into the soil of this
deep, dark gleaming
earth.

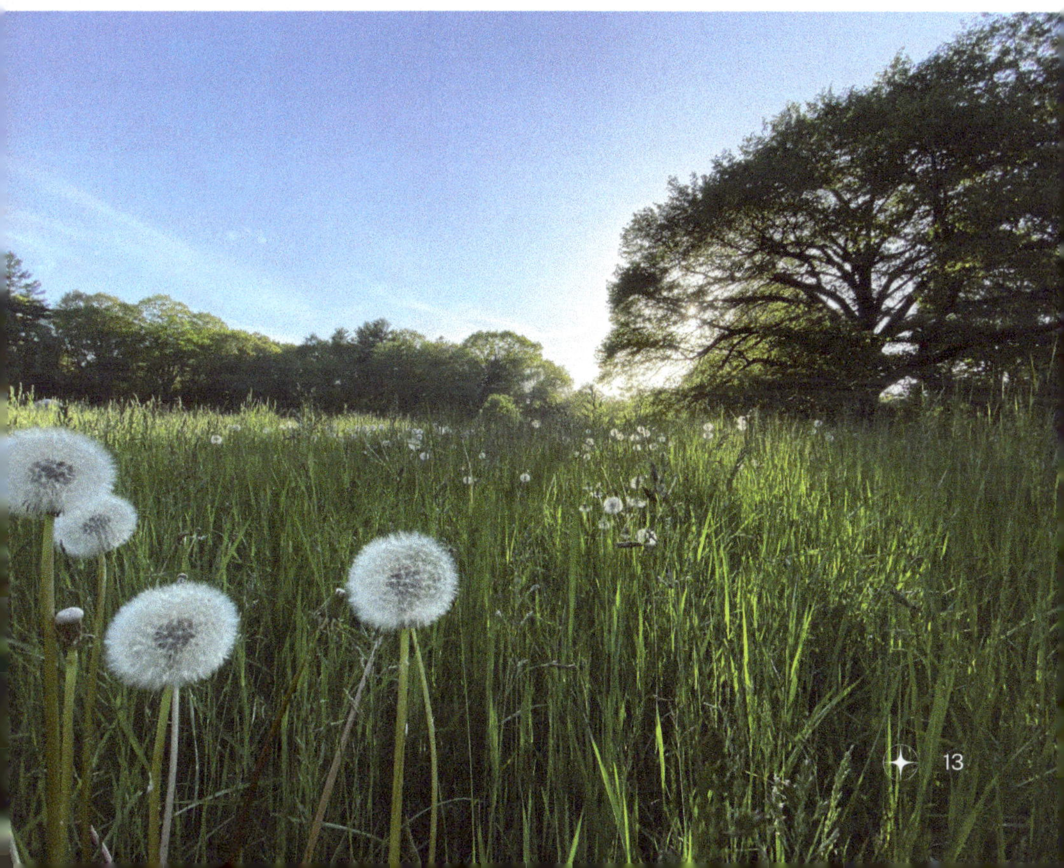

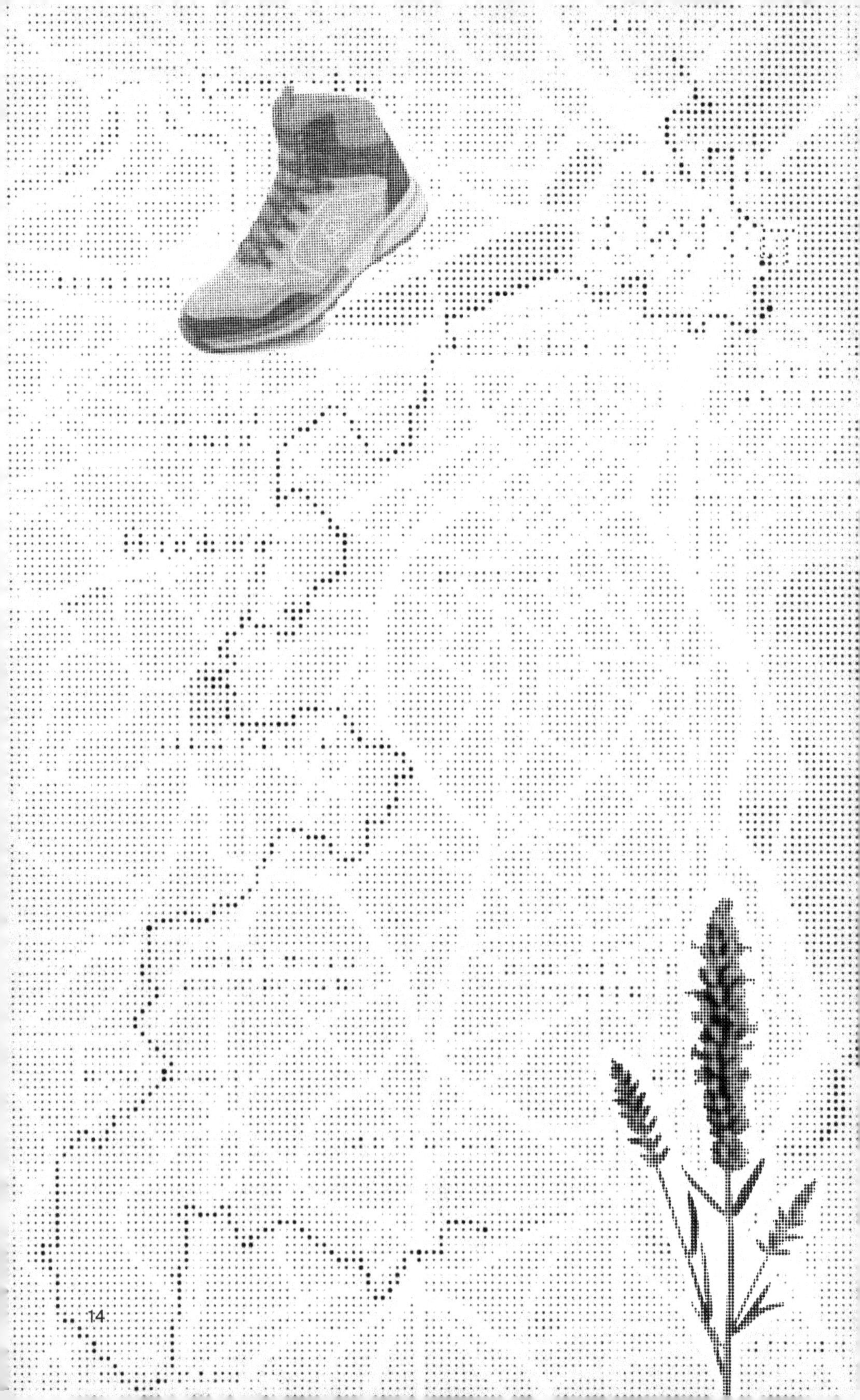

WALKING ACROSS BOSTON

The Q sat down with urban trail builder, Miles Howard, to discuss his process of stitching together a 27-mile "Walking City Trail."

The Quinobequin Review (QR): We should probably start here: what is urban trail building?

Miles Howard (MH): Urban trail building is the process of stitching together existing pathways to create a continuous trail. Instead of building a trail from scratch, it is a way of curating a city's walkable spaces.

QR: How did you end up in Boston? Did you grow up here?

MH: I grew up in Winchester but I feel like I came of age in Boston because we had a commuter rail station in town. As soon as my parents would let me ride the train, I would go into Boston and just roam. I would go to parks, international restaurants that we didn't have in Winchester, weird bookstores, fashion stores, sex stores, you name it. It was a much wider world than the suburbs. After college I ended up back in Boston, covering nightlife and event listings for the *Boston Phoenix*, a newspaper that folded in 2012.

QR: Did reporting on Boston's nightlife change your perspective on the city?

MH: Boston has, I think, knowingly cultivated this buttoned-up image. But working for the Phoenix, I found hidden pockets of nightlife that didn't really fit this tidy, conservative sensibility. These underground scenes are becoming more endangered, but back before the cops had really cracked down, you could still find your way into a basement show somewhere in Allston without having to be plugged into all the right subreddits. These grungy, vibrant parts of Boston made me fall in love with the city in a new way. There is plenty of creative life happening underground here, and sometimes it comes to the surface. I think that urban trail building falls under that umbrella of things happening off the mainstream radar.

QR: Is that what inspired you to start the walking trail?

MH: It's funny. The part about building a subculture came later, but at the beginning it was really just about finding green space. I've always liked hiking; I grew up spending a lot of time in the White Mountains, and in college I spent the summers working for the

Appalachian Mountain Club as a crew member in their high mountain huts. In 2022, I hiked San Francisco's Crosstown Trail, and I thought, "I could do this in Boston." The San Francisco trail was basically a patchwork of preexisting paths and parks connected with interesting street walks to form this epic 17-mile public-transit-accessible hike. I remember scrolling around Google Maps in the airport on the way home, trying to envision how I could make it work here.

QR: What are some of the highlights of the trail?

MH: There's a fun spot in Roslindale called Fairy Hollow. The trail goes right by a community garden called the Sherman Street Greenspace Conservancy, and inside there's a little mailbox where kids can leave a letter for the fairies, and the fairies will write them back.

But my favorite section is probably the Arnold Arboretum because it's a sanctuary in the middle of Boston. I remember when the *Boston Phoenix* was starting to fold and the atmosphere was getting pretty grim with layoffs, I realized I needed to find my next thing. I was feeling a bit panicked, and I went for a walk through the center of Arboretum, through all those huge evergreen conifers. Walking through the trees, I understood that I needed to stay committed to writing in some way. And that's when I started freelancing. I've been on subsequent walks there that have helped me make other big decisions about life, work, relationships, you name it. It's always helped me when I needed it.

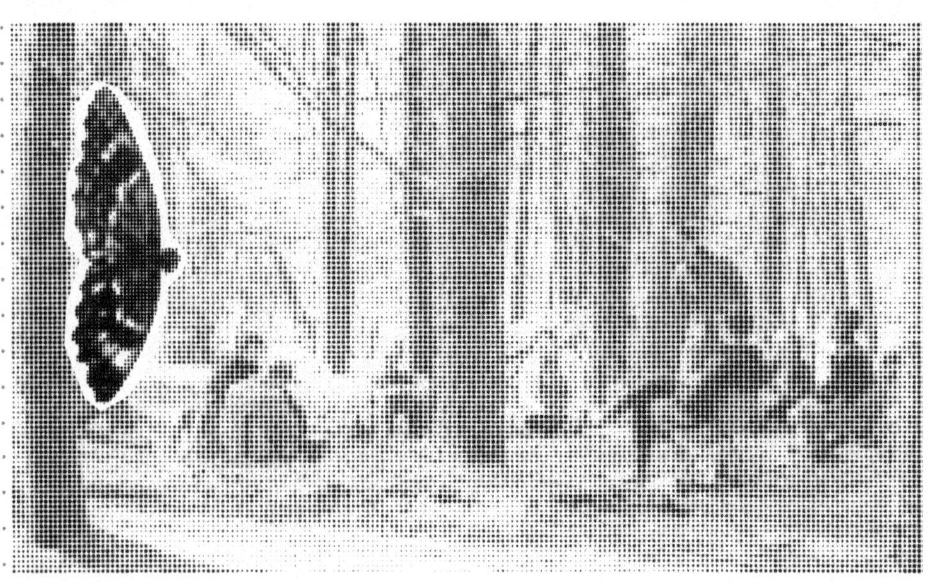

QR: Did any sections of the trail surprise you?

MH: Yes, I knew about this big staircase going up the back side of Mission Hill, but I assumed it just led to a road on a higher street. I didn't realize that it led to a second staircase that serves as a kind of throughway to access all of these houses that were stacked tightly up the hillside. At the top of the second staircase, there's a path that leads through the McLaughlin Woods Urban Wild, and finally to the summit, where there is a little orchard. It was such a cool moment because I never would've known about this if I had just relied on my preliminary map.

When I was first planning the trail, those stairs did not appear on AllTrails or any maps. But now they do, and I think it's because enough people have walked the route with their GPS tracking activated, that these open-source street maps now recognize a walkable path. It's a nice example of the ripple effects of urban hiking.

QR: Why do you think urban hiking resonates with so many people?

MH: When I was planning the route, I shared some teasers on my social media accounts. I remember putting out a photo of that hidden Mission Hill staircase, and thousands of people liked and shared it. That's when I thought, "woah, we might be tapping into something here." I think there's something so timeless and romantic to people about finding adventure out your back door. In the Hobbit, Bilbo literally steps right out of his front door and is whisked away to a world beyond. I think the Walking City Trail gives people access to a hidden world in Boston, fully walkable and blooming with life. I also think that sewing hidden connections between seemingly disparate spaces has a lot of power, especially in a city shaped by such intense racial and economic separation.

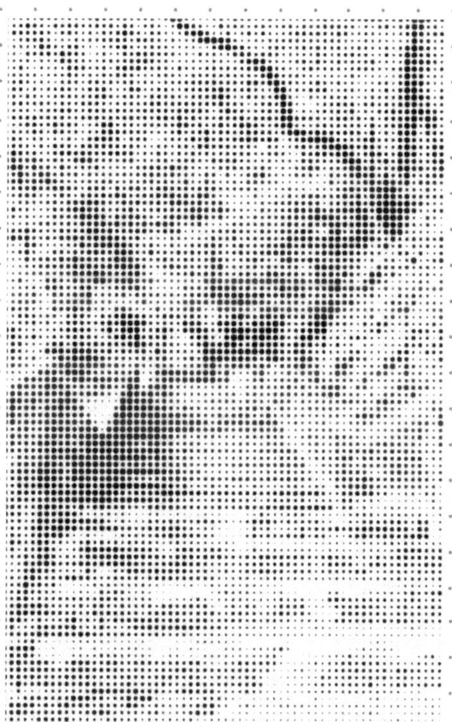

QR: Can you give me an example of a section of the trail that seems to bridge two separate worlds?

MH: There's a spot between Mattapan and Hyde Park where you can really see the boundary between neighborhoods. The trail begins in Mattapan, which is bustling with lots of busy road crossings and activity. From there, you enter this much lesser known green space called the Edgewater Greenway, a snarled patch of woods along the riverside with a "desire path" cutting through it (desire paths are unofficial footpaths, marked by foot traffic but unrecognized by park planners). So you follow the path, brushing past vines, climbing over a few downed trees, and finally you huff your way over a short stone wall and you're suddenly in Hyde Park, which is a much more suburban landscape compared to the urban density of Mattapan Square.

There's another spot called Nira Rock that sits on the boundary of a totally wild and urban environment. It is this huge pudding stone boulder, the size of a house, that sits right up against the back of the Jamaica Plain Veteran's Hospital. There are trees on one side and tons of dense residential buildings on the other.

QR: How has the trail changed over time?

MH: The trail used to be much shorter. I was able to extend it by expanding my definition of what it means to be an "immersive space." My friend Matthew Brody pointed out that the fourth part of the trail (which goes through downtown Boston) felt rushed. I was looking for green spaces, which downtown doesn't really have a lot of, so I was trying to move through that section as quickly as possible.

So I really challenged myself to find pockets of that section that were immersive in other ways. The Boston Harbor, for example, isn't very green, but its definitely an immersive space. The Leather District, which is Boston's tiniest

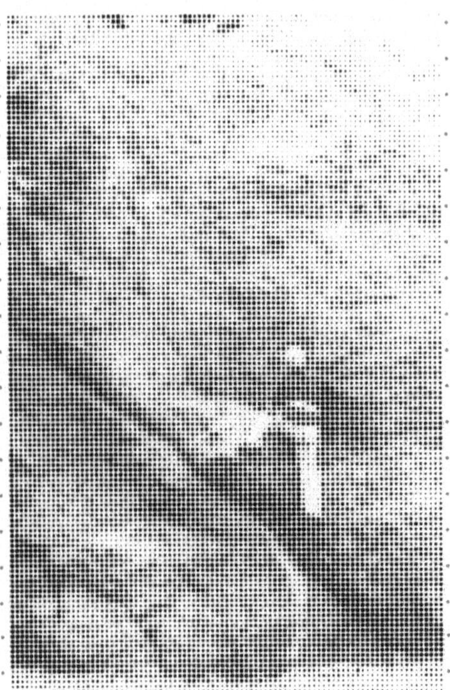

URBAN CLIMBING AT NIRA ROCK, PATCH.COM

neighborhood, has really interesting architecture. Martin's Park has this elevated figure-eight shaped path through the best playground in Boston.

QR: You recently walked the entire 90-mile perimeter of Boston. Are you going to make this a formal urban trail?

I would be lying if I said that thought hadn't crossed my mind. I'm not quite ready to spill the details yet, but I have two ideas in mind as sequels for the Walking City Trail. One is the perimeter loop. The other is a different route into Boston, moving from west to east, as an alternative to the original south to north route.

A GUIDE TO URBAN TRAIL BUILDING:

1. DECIDE ON IF IT'S A GROUP OR SOLO ENDEAVOR. MAPPING A TRAIL ALONE IS FAST, BUT WORKING TOGETHER MEANS IT WILL CONTINUE TO EXIST IF YOU GROW TIRED OF PROMOTING IT ALONE

2. PICK A THEME. THE WALKING CITY TRAIL THEME IS IMMERSIVE SPACES; YOURS COULD BE BARS THAT A-LIST CELEBRITIES HAVE BEEN THROWN OUT OF EITHER WAY, A THEMATIC COMPASS HELPS.

3. CREATE A SPECULATIVE MAP. MILES USES ALLTRAILS BECAUSE IT SHOWS WALKABLE SPACES.

4. WALK THE TRAIL + ADJUST ACCORDINGLY. WHAT IS THE MOST INTERESTING ROUTE IRL?

5. CREATE GUIDED RESOURCES. THE WALKING CITY TRAIL HAS A WEBSITE, DIGITAL MAP, TURN-BY-TURN DIRECTIONS FOR SECONDARY NAVIGATION, AND SIGNAGE FOR PEOPLE WHO ORGANICALLY ENCOUNTER THE TRAIL.

6. GET THE WORD OUT. PROMOTE ON SOCIAL CHANNELS, LOCAL MEDIA, ETC. SO PEOPLE CAN FIND IT!

STEPS FOR STARTING YOUR OWN TRAIL, FROM CONVERSATION WITH MILES

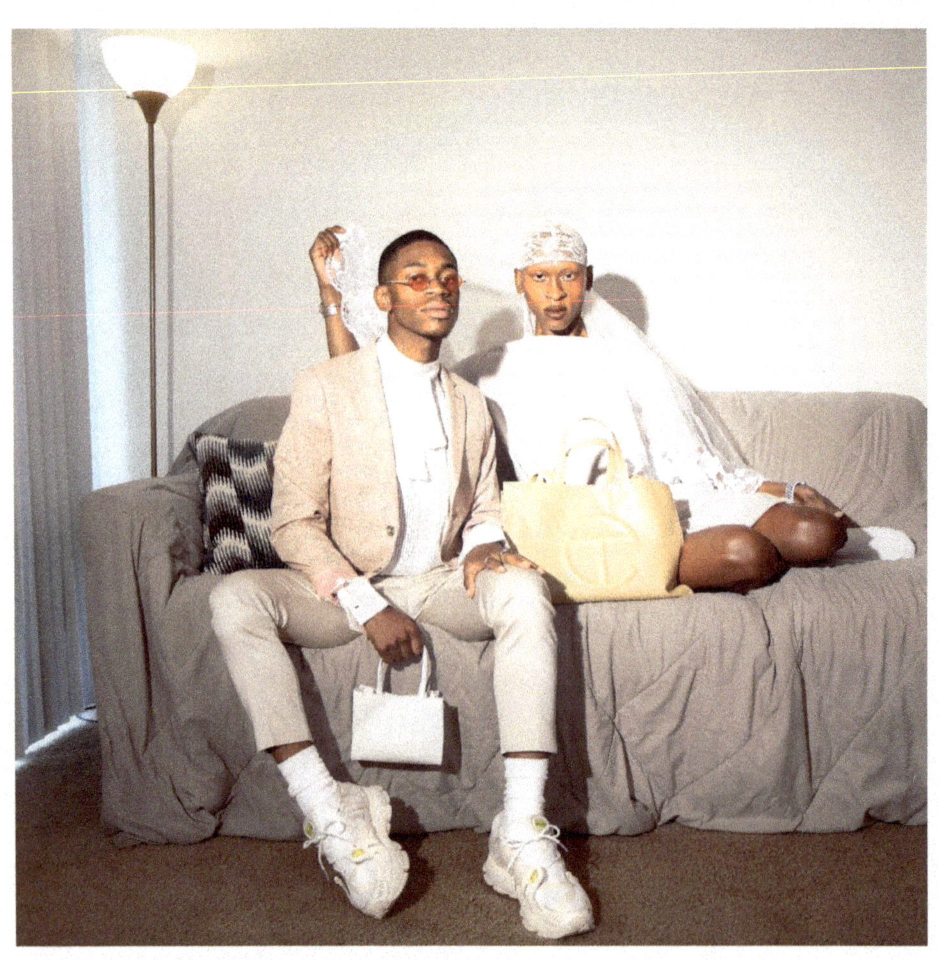

TWINS BE OMNISCIENT LIKE LIGHT — GOLDEN

RUNAWAY BRIDE

ERWIN KAMUENE: Last summer, I moved into a new apartment with my partner. It was on the first floor of an old building boxed around a courtyard knee deep in flowers that looked like fried eggs. It had two official rooms - a small bed and living room - perpendicular to a hallway bridging the bathroom to the kitchen. We began the decoration process quite impulsively, starting with records sourced from a local share-shelf that we piled atop a broken turntable. They were Reggae, House, and RnB records, shoved into greasy sleeves sporting 99 cent stickers all over. We grabbed whatever else we found on the streets, debated the merits of a tattered rocking chair as a work of art, and stacked used poetry collections on the windowsills. It all came together when the bed and futon arrived, and after burning many bushels of incense to cleanse the apartment of the lingering smell of stale cigarettes.

This happened during a part of summer we crudely named "the dying season", for the number of ambulances that ricocheted to and from the nursing home right next to us. Their peals were like jolts of electricity stranding us in soggy puddles of awakeness, which rarely mattered to us anyway since our dream was a waking one. It was strolling beneath paper lanterns in Little Saigon, people watching at Arlington, and sitting in the pavilion at Carson Beach watching airplanes arc across the sky. It was the many nights when after she'd return from the butcher shop having waded ankle deep in pig viscera, would leave her pants to dry on the bedpost and assume an odalisque in sweats from the night before.

In moments like these we'd think of our place in Boston, which we defined as a city that took as much as it gave. A city that always accommodated ambition, which we knew by a neighbor who routinely got up at 1 a.m. to spend the night picking rat brains at Harvard Med. It was a city beholden to its institutions, meaning it was a city of careerism and promotions and whole apartments strewn onto sidewalks once they'd served their purpose. A home within the midst of this, even if just a tiny one bedroom with a consumptive radiator, seemed a place in which we could fortify ourselves — a foraging hole for the surviving bits of tribute that sustained our relationship.

—

Around this time, I went to the Gardner Museum to see an exhibition of photographs from Golden, a queer artist that I admire. The portraits — of themself and many friends — were taken

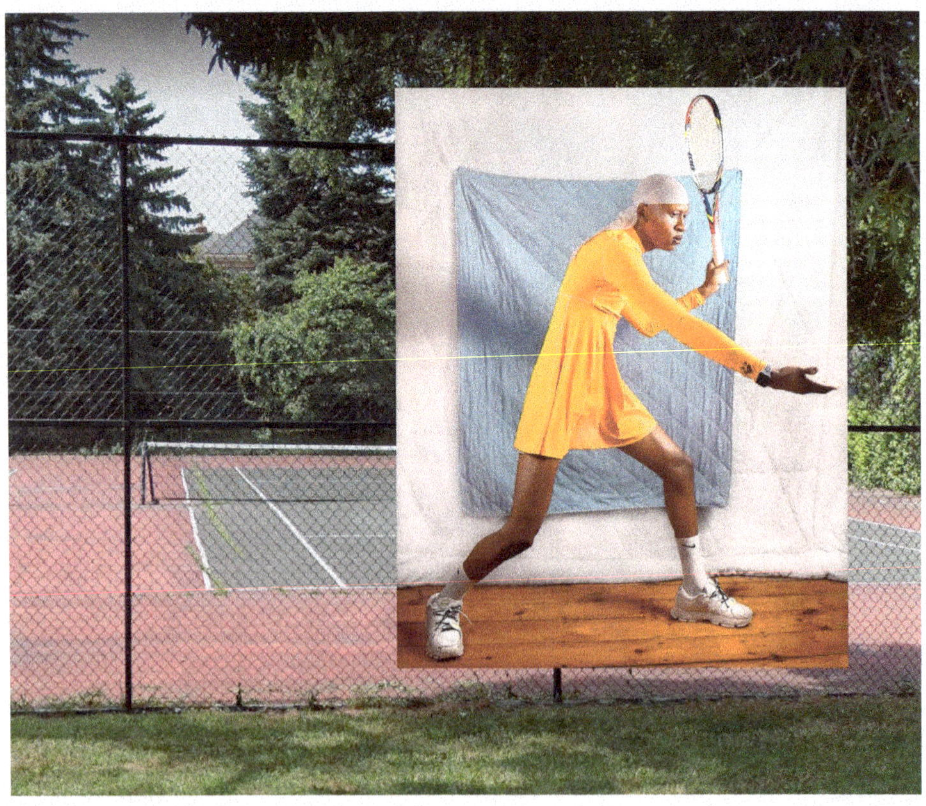

in bedrooms, living rooms, and porch banisters demarcating the boundaries of these safe and open spaces. They were as warm as old covers of Seventeen, but were also redolent of sadness. One particular piece - a portrait of the artist superimposed over a tennis court, titled "I just want to wear my orange dress to the tennis courts and come back unbothered" - imbued me with a sense of doubt about the legitimacy of our own fantasy of four walls and a roof.

While the pictures showed the potential of home as a space for liberation as ours was for us, I couldn't jettison the contradiction inherent in finite liberty, in freedom strapped in a corset. Perhaps "sanctuaries" was a better term to describe these spaces, but one still fraught with feelings of claustrophobia. That in an omitted version, the banisters were transformed into bales of chicken wire that pricked instead of caressed the seat of their sweatpants. The photos planted the idea that while the world tries to assail our interiors, it equally chafes against our own yearnings. And though in the meantime, we lounged like hippos in mud, I feared our stasis would inevitably dissolve at both the city's as well as our own behest.

A fragment of poetry from the windowsills:

. . . but isn't it because by dissolving like so
much dust into the sheets we are crowding
south, into the kitchen, into
nowhere?

- Denis Johnson, "Quickly Aging Here".

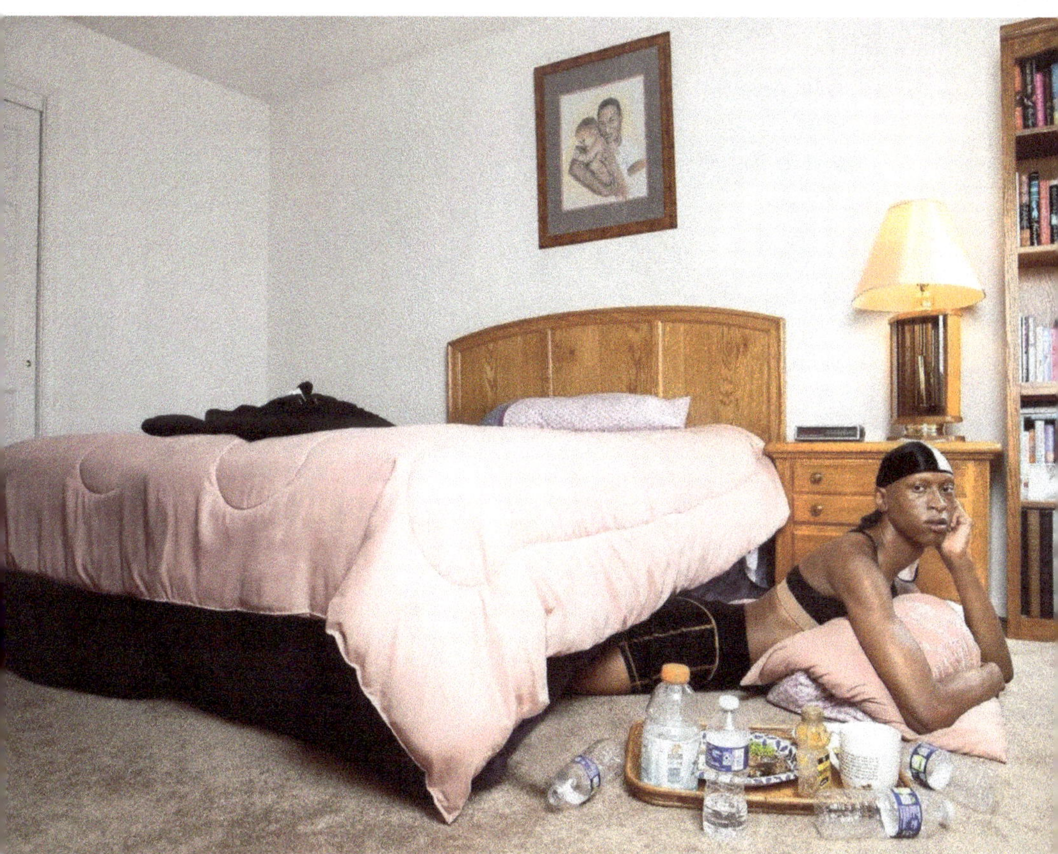

One day we decided to forgo our usual spots and went to lunch at a franchise whose Boston location we wanted to try. We ran into our neighbor on the way out, who was eager to talk about the ambulance problem. He told us it was the lights that bothered him more than the sirens, and said something about how the eerie ones with lights but no sirens were carting dead patients to the hospital. At the restaurant, we got into an argument and I could barely stomach the bougie addition of onions to my chicken and waffles. We went to Arlington for a palette cleanser and while sitting on a bench trying to look like a couple, encountered the tail end of a wedding procession passing in front of us.

The middle-aged bride was in a white satin dress, wrestling with the train attached to her bun. Every few feet it would drag on the pavement, slightly tipping her ajar before she adjusted her footing. We could tell the wedding was hastily put together, by the flock of groomsmen loitering at the fountain, by her stolid mother escorting her down the aisle, and by her blase attitude as if the ceremony was a rite that impeded something more important. When she got near the bench, she asked my partner to help lift the train, which she did, struggling to keep up with the bride.

Despite our better judgment, the ceremony lifted our spirits and we couldn't help but get swept away in the fanfare. I immediately thought of the ending of The Graduate, when Dustin Hoffman passionately steals Katherine Ross from the wedding altar. In the film, their dreams only get them as far as the back of a Greyhound before reality sets in and the screen fades to black. Here, it got these two lovers to the dingy corner of a public park just outside the range of a pissing Cupid. Who knows how far it would get us?

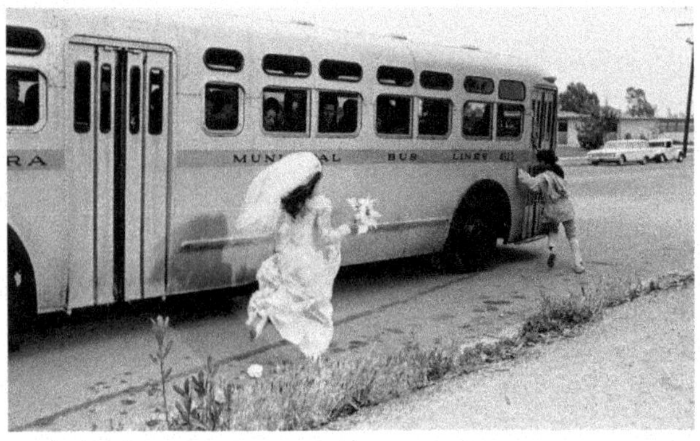

THE GRADUATE, 1967

NEIGHBORHOOD PORTRAITS

BY TWO NOBLE AND GREENOUGH HIGH SCHOOL STUDENTS

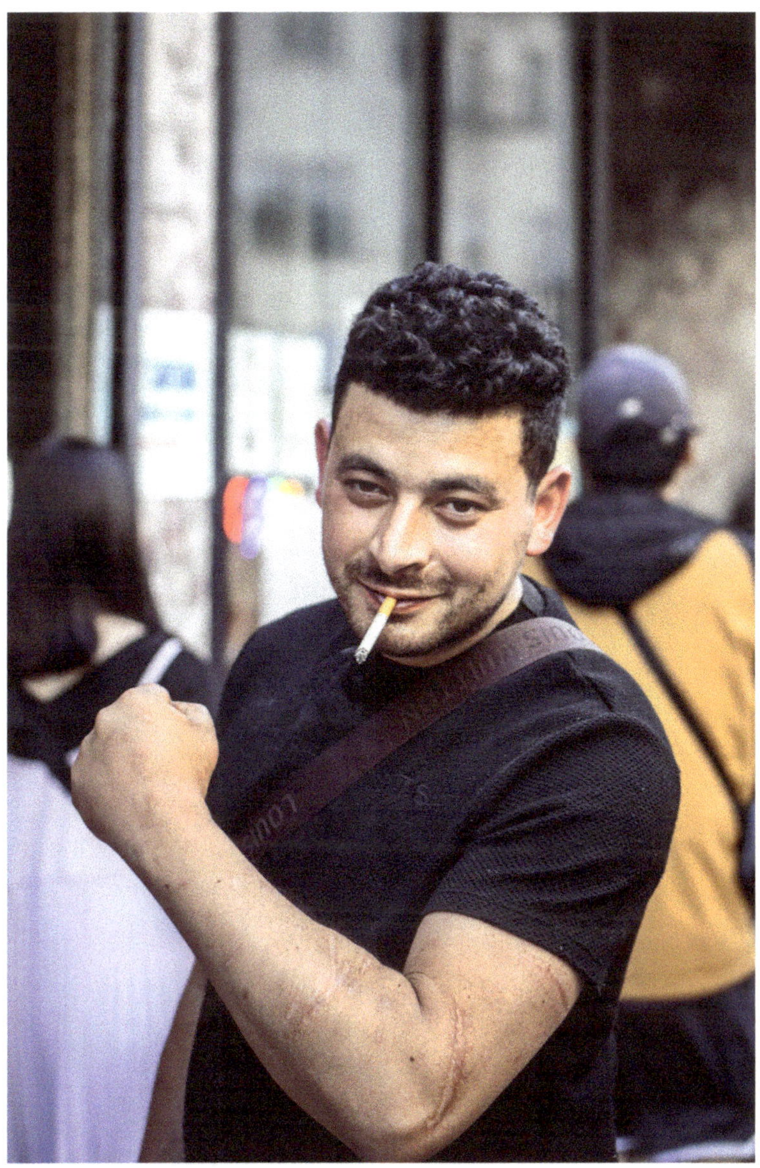

MAN ON BEACH STREET, CHINATOWN, BY TAHIRA MUHAMMAD

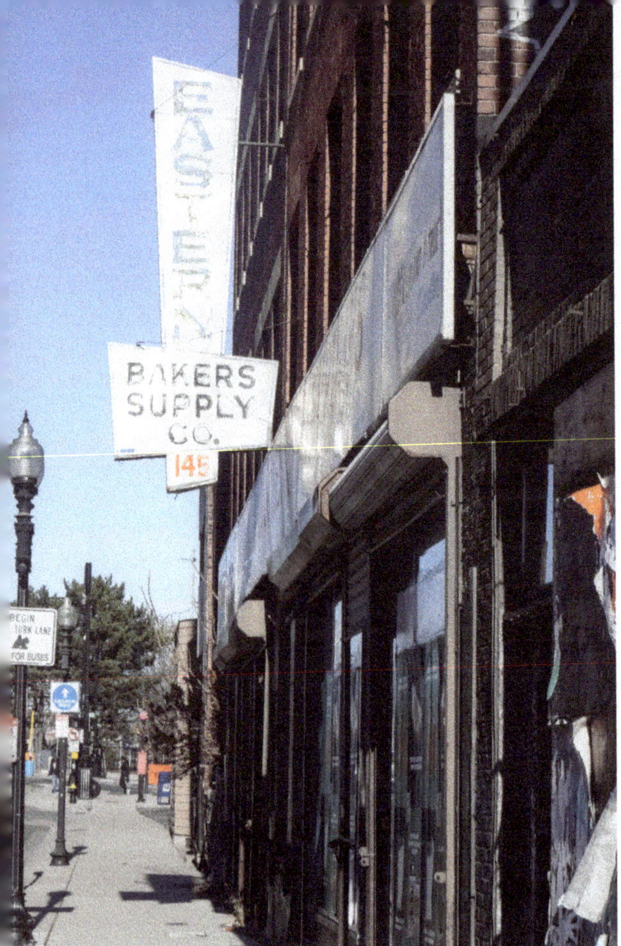

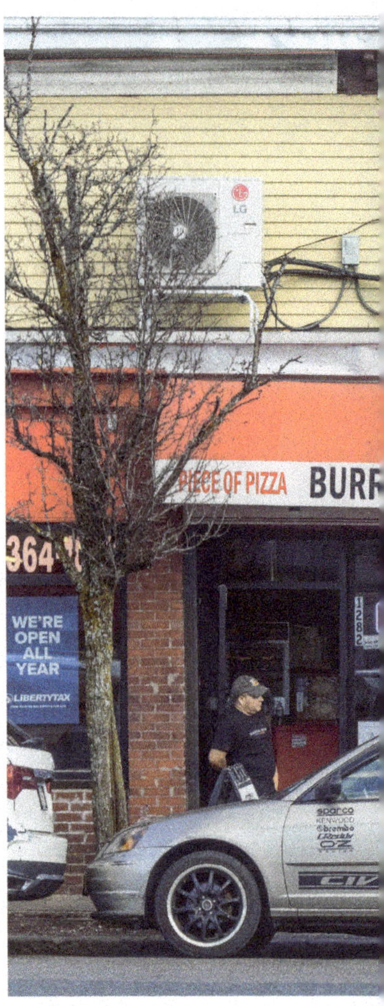

TAHIRA MUHAMMAD: The enduring nature of aged storefronts, the always open Simcos on American Legion Highway for a late-night snack, spice shopping in Little Italy for the freshest oregano, the outpour of students onto the corners right at 2:30 when schools dismiss, all of which are part of my city's fabric. The delicate gestures and daily routines that go unnoticed but speak volumes about a community fascinate me.

I examine these details with the precision of a magnifying glass. Creating my own document of day-to-day scenes that feature the lives of people around me in the city I call home. Having spent much of my life as a spectator from the confines of a car, I am driven by a deep-seated curiosity to explore and get closer. Walking the streets and looking for moments that reveal specific people, places, and times show the true essence of Boston. The beauty, culture, and bustle of it all combine to make up the city I've learned to love. Even though a lingering tension lies, breaking down those barriers that inhibit connection allows for a mission of exploration. I'm finding my city, my favorite views, the neighborhoods I tour, the people I meet, and the restaurants I eat at. In my story, I create a unique cast of characters and settings composed of all things that move me. This is the city I love. This is my Boston.

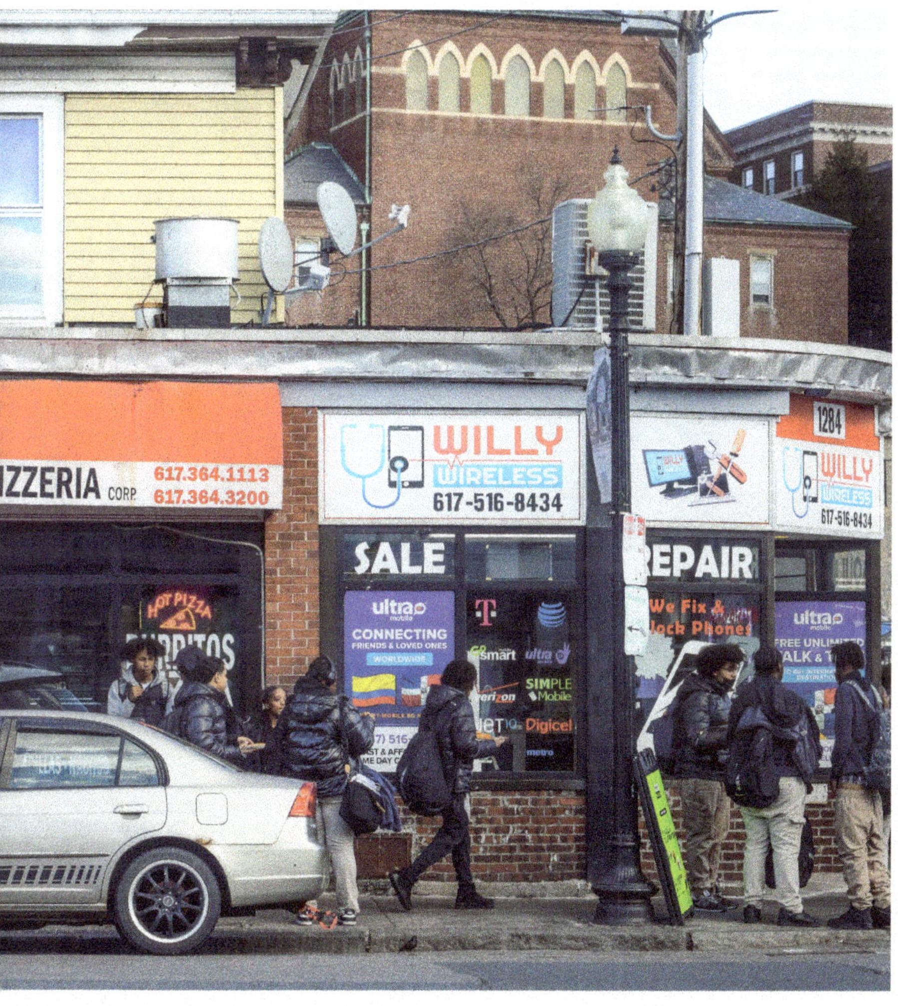

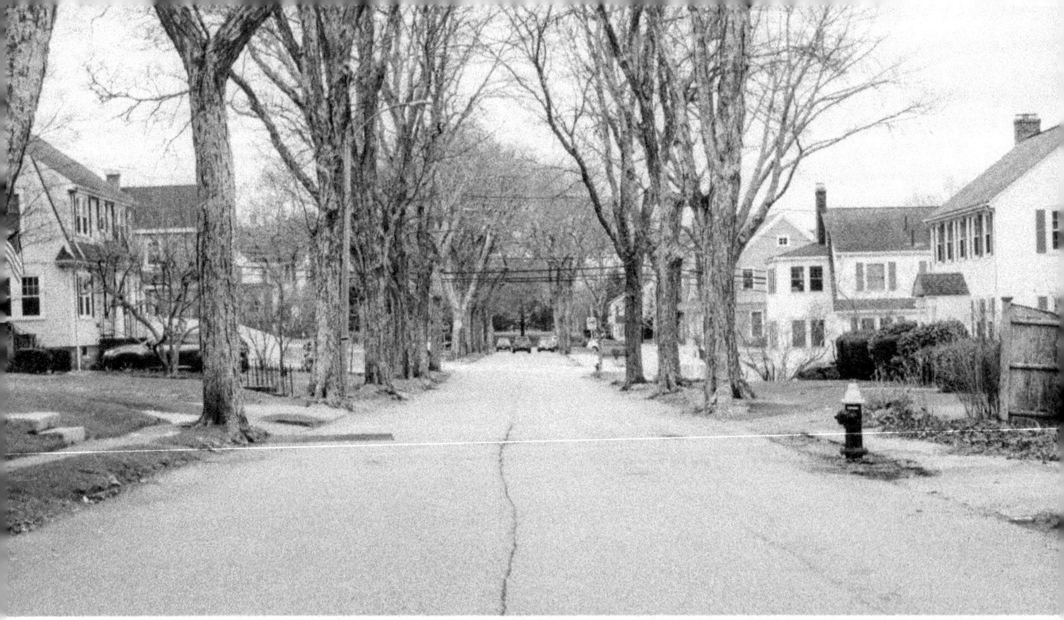

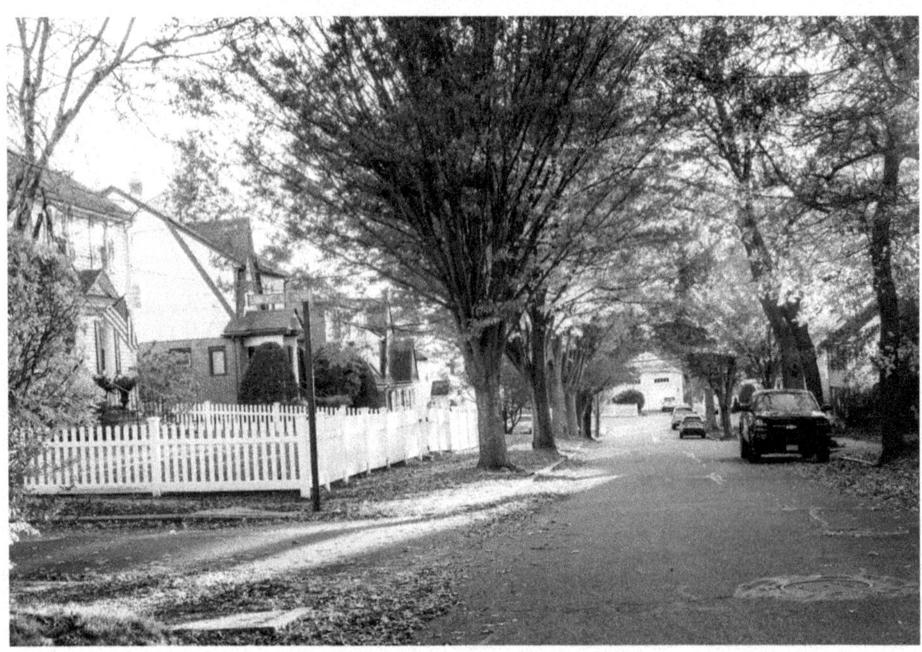

SAM LINBERG: Growing up, like most kids, my friends and I walked and biked around our neighborhood to pass the time or to get from place to place. We had parameters of where we could go. Naturally, we could only be within a few minutes walk of any of our houses. I can vividly remember walking the same path everyday after school with my friends from my neighborhood. On that walk home from school, we saw the same people day in and day out walking their dogs or going for a run. Now, when I walk or drive down those same roads, there are new routines, and

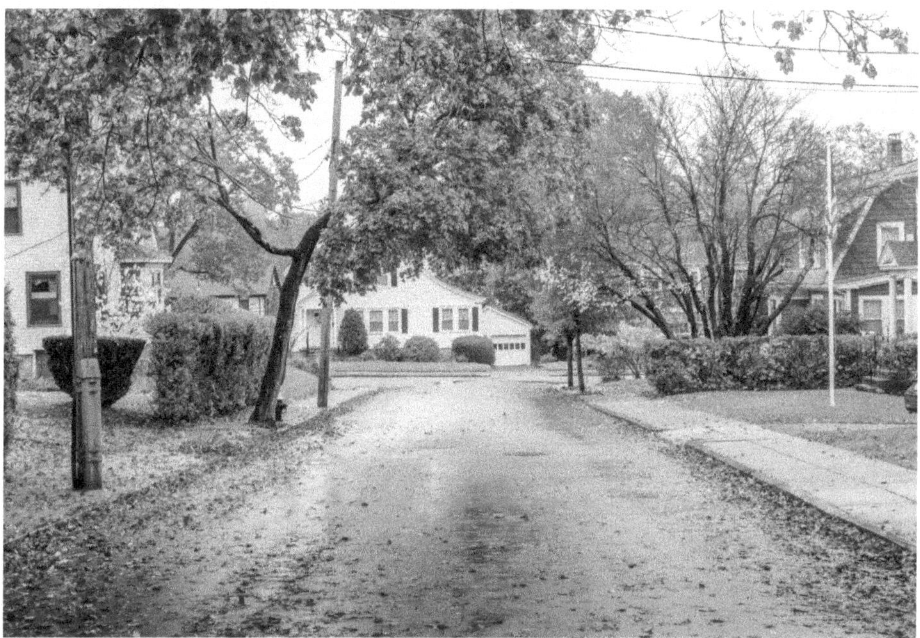

new people that I see following them. These streets that I used to walk on everyday with my friends, I drive on now, and I still see the same people everyday. These streets bring a sense of nostalgia to me, as I still have a lot of those same friends today, and I still see Jack's house where we used to play basketball, my old bus stop on the corner of Oriole and Wren, the water tower up the street where we have been walking the dogs since I was little. We still live in the same neighborhood, but we are not the little kids that we once were.

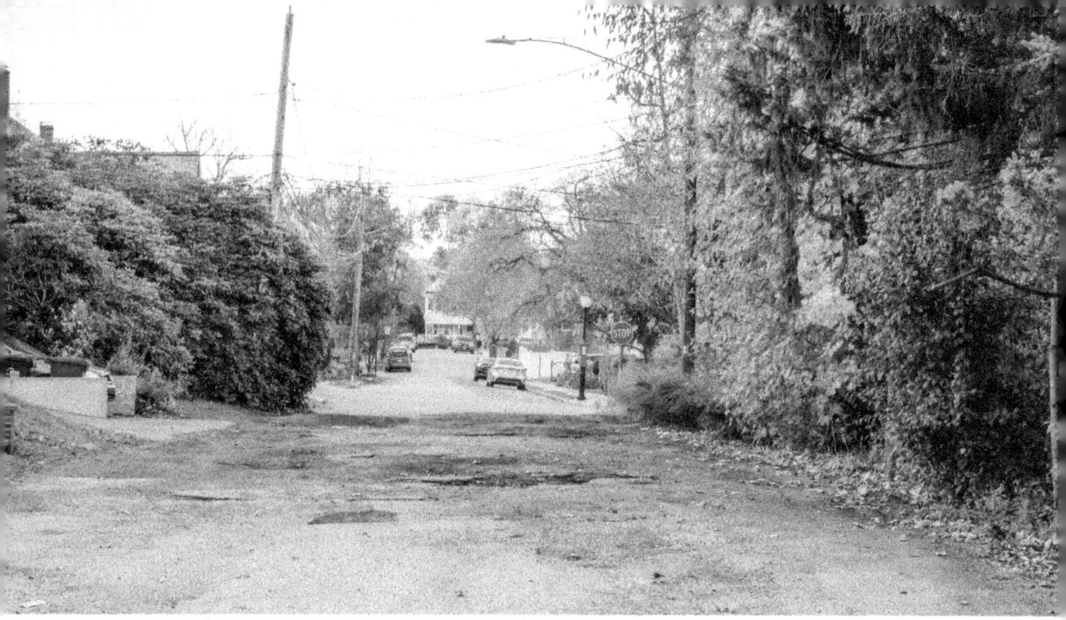

A NEW PERSPECTIVE ON THE HARBOR

ABBEY CAHILL: Courageous Sailing found Rich Odell at the perfect time. Rich, who grew up in Framingham in the 80s, had a tough childhood. "My parents didn't really know how to be parents, and I ended up in a psychiatric hospital when I was really young." After an incident involving a stolen lawnmower and some hacked-up bushes, he had a chance to start fresh.

Rich's probation officer, Carl Gomes, got him into Glenhaven Academy, a therapeutic boarding school for teens in Marlborough. Gomes also organized a sailing program through the county's juvenile probation department and Boston's Courageous Sailing Center. The mission behind Courageous Sailing — which has evolved over the years to include people of all ages, backgrounds, and abilities — was to make sailing accessible for people who didn't know they needed it. "You're going sailing tomorrow," Gomes told Rich one day. It was a command, not a question.

For three summers, Rich boarded the bus at the Marlborough Courthouse and headed into Charlestown. In the mornings, Rich and his peers had class inside the octagonal walls of the Muster House. They ate bagged lunch at a water park on the pier (now The Anchor beer garden), then they rigged up the R19s and went sailing.

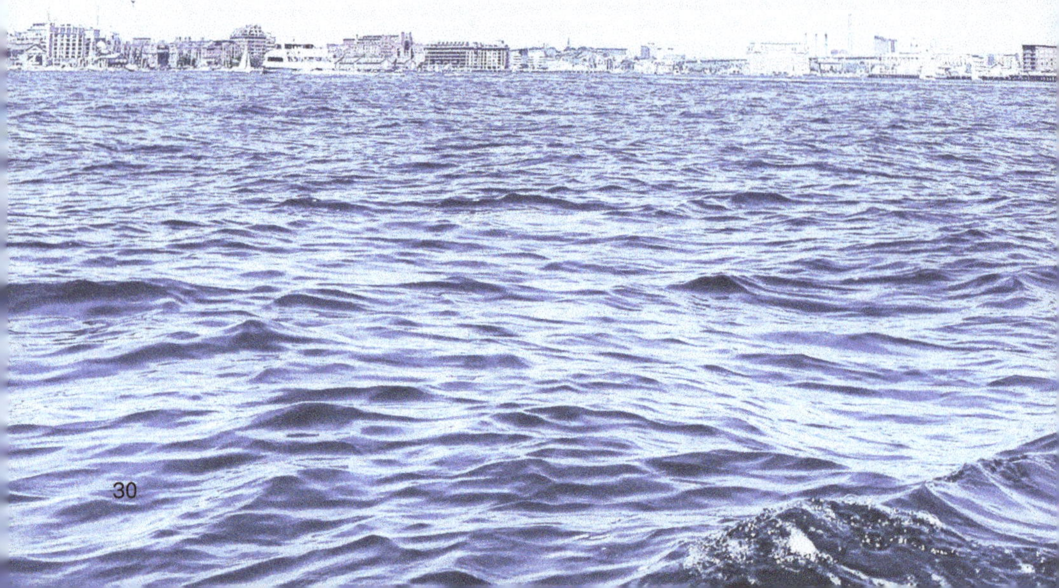

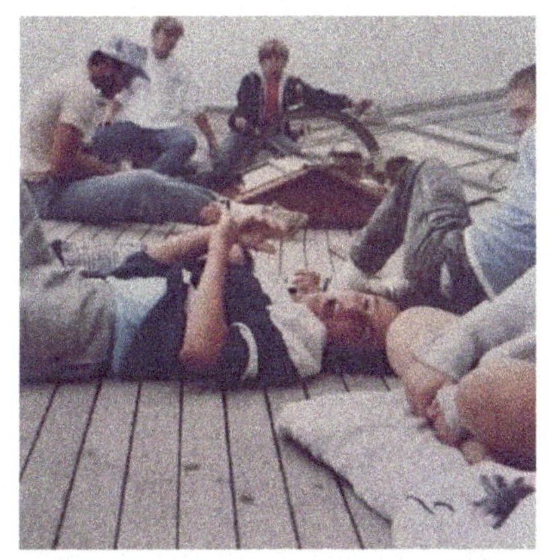

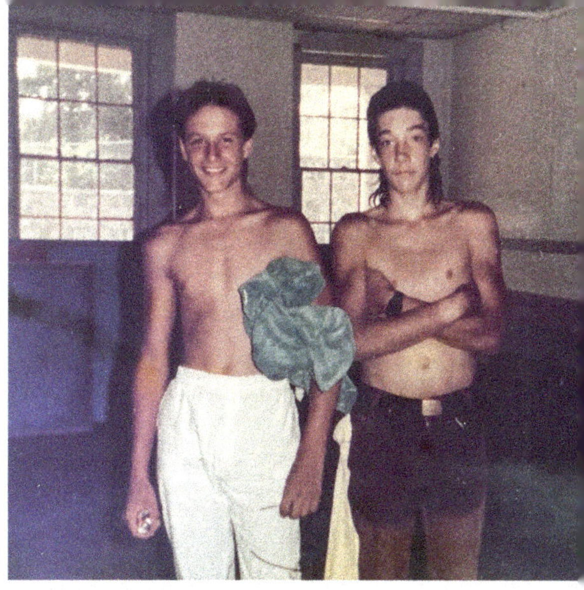

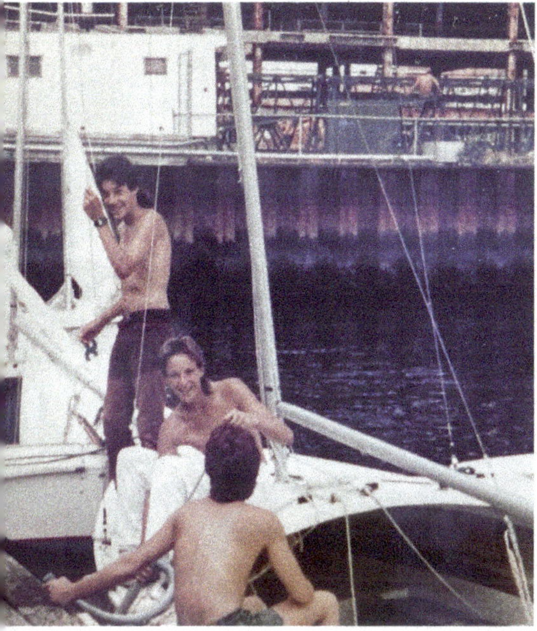

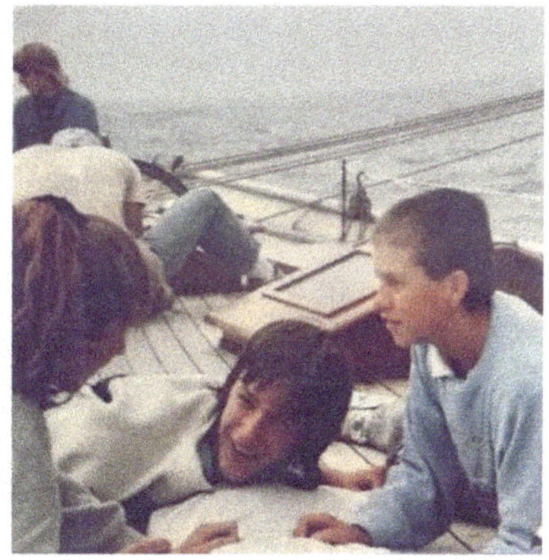

I had no money. I had no friends. I had no home. I really missed out on a childhood. But sailing got me out and gave me something different. While everyone else was doing their thing, going off to school, I was going fucking sailing. It was total freedom. When I look at the pictures, I can see I wasn't worried about anything when I was sailing.

I first spoke to Rich on a Tuesday before Memorial Day weekend. I asked him to describe what it feels like to sail on the harbor, but he insisted that some things are not easily explained. "Come with me this Saturday," he offered.

I met Rich at 9 AM in the Charlestown Navy Yard, and we retraced his old walk from the bus stop to the Courageous Sailing pier (which looks "pretty much the same.") At 10, we met Jen Bodde, Courageous' Director of Education who'd agreed to take us out. By 11, we were tacking out of the harbor.

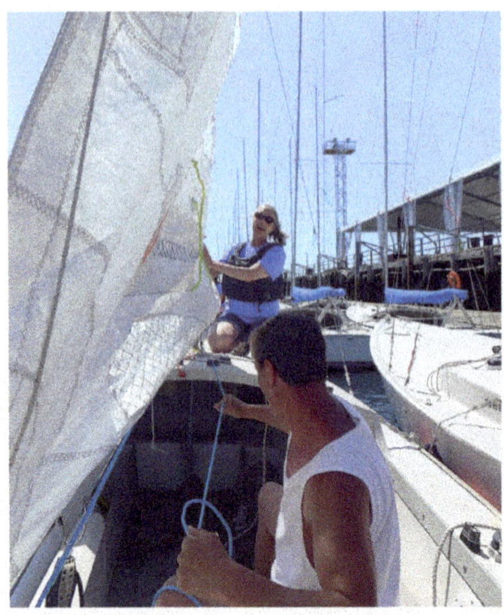

From the water, Boston unfurls in one continuous line. Our often disjointed city—divided by bridges and tunnels and thick traffic snarls—is instantly made smaller. East Boston is just 400 yards to Charlestown, and Charlestown is just 300 yards to the North End. Courageous founder Harry Mc-

Donough saw the unifying power of the harbor: "Learning sailing on the harbor, which touches all the neighborhoods, can bring them together."

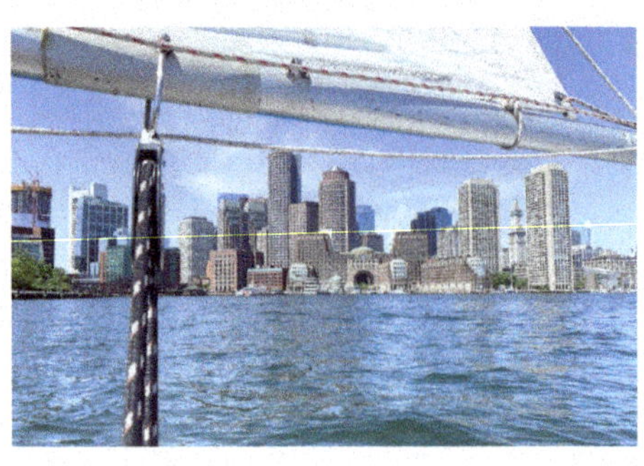

As we sail south, red-bricked downtown becomes glossy new Seaport becomes industrial South Boston becomes green Castle Island, where dozens of sunbathers scatter the lawn. On the other side of the channel is the airport, and the planes fly low over our boat. Rich wants to know if I imagined it this way. "Not at all," I tell him. It feels like the whole city is out here.

A Boston Electric Boat carries a sequined jazz band making a music video. Almost anyone can rent these boats, which explains their tendency to happily drift through Courageous racecourses. The CODZILLA boat, marked with two yellow eyes and a toothy grimace, makes hairpin turns across the harbor, sending water spraying, hair flying, and a hundred tiny hands into the air, screaming with delight. Reminders of a violent world float quietly along the docks. Here is the USS Constitution, witness to the War of

1812 Here is the USS Cassin Young, a World War II destroyer, survivor of two Kamikaze hits. Here is an unsailable Tall Ship, masts askew, hauled down from Nova Scotia to make the perfect backdrop for sipping Aperol spritzes. Beside it is an Astroturf lounge with Nantucket-themed tables. Here are the power boaters in their summer pastels, wives laying out on the bows, yellow labs sniffing the breeze, American flags flying straight back. A cruise ship departs (1 beep = "We are off!"). A tanker issues a warning (5 beeps = "Make your intentions clear, little boat. I'm trying not to hit you!")

Beneath all the commotion, Rich and Jen can read the harbor like a map. Where I see a wide swath of choppy blue, they see pockets of wind and dead zones, the "Lower Middle" where boats run aground, the "washing machine" where the no-wake zone ends, the invisible place where a tunnel carries cars beneath us, and another where the current shifts and the Charles River is pumped out to sea.

On our way back to the Navy Yard, we pass a Courageous instructor teaching a lesson, sitting on the edge of the hull while a student steers. The magic of sailing, Rich and Jen concur, is paying attention. And everyone notices something different. Jen often sails with someone on the autism spectrum who loves the wake that the ferries leave behind. "It opened my mind to how it might feel to have sensory differences," she says. "It's like sailing through seltzer." Recently, she took out a radio host who was most interested in the sounds, recording the click click click of rope through a pulley block and the rhythmic clanking of the rigging against the mast. Others notice the physical sensations; Rich once took a group of blind people sailing, and they all felt the wind on their faces.

But for Rich, it has always been about freedom. Later that day, he sends me a clip of an interview with Christopher Cross on the meaning of his song, "Sailing." As a teenager, Cross escaped his dysfunctional home through sailing:

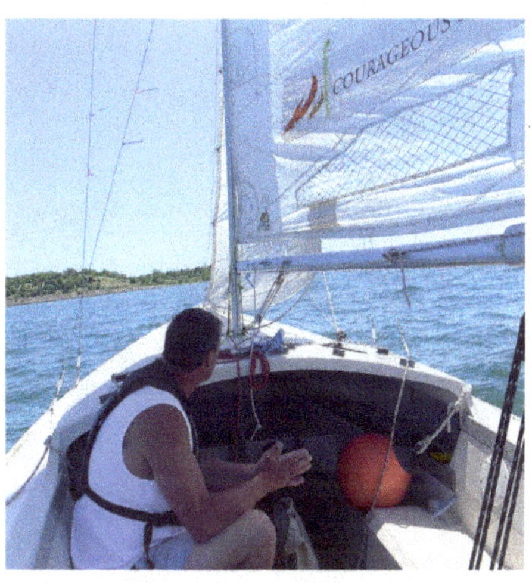

Sailing / Takes me away to where I've always heard it could be / Just a dream and the wind to carry me / Soon I will be free!

STREET-SCAPE CURATOR

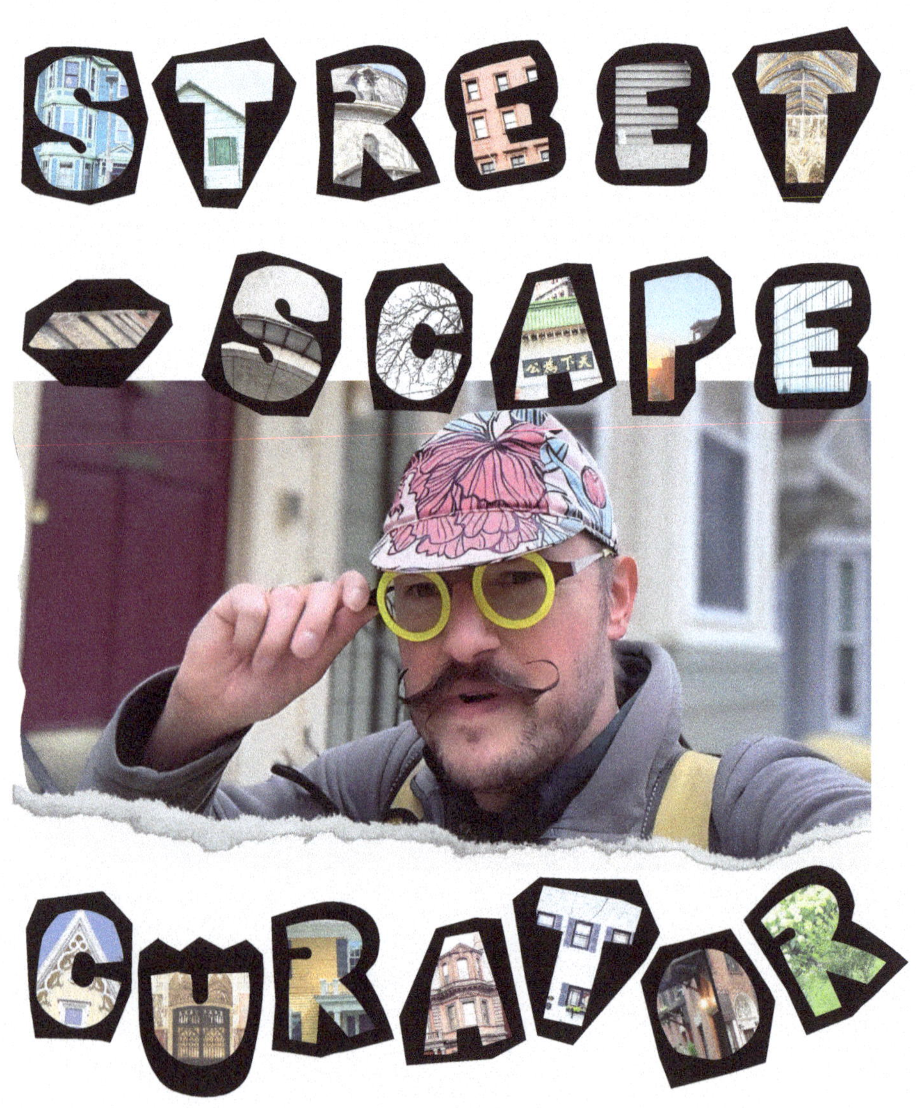

Artist, cyclist, and Dorchester resident showcases
three curiosities from Boston's former life

MATTHEW DICKEY: Cows don't make roads. They never have and never will. People do. And people have made criss-crossing paths for thousands of years. Shawmut was the name given to the area where the Mystic, Charles, and Neponset Rivers meet. Today we call it Boston. It's a tangle of roads first made by Native people weaving between drumlins and walking along streams. To say cows shaped the streets of Boston is to ignore thousands of years of human history.

I'm not an architect or an urban planner. Nor am I a developer. But as a Streetscape Curator, I am simultaneously all of those things. To be a Streetscape Curator is to be curious about your surroundings. It is to question how spaces make you feel and why they look the way they do. Who were they built for? Who were they built by? It's also a way of questioning what history has been erased, who erased it, and what remains.

Today, Boston is a city shaped by humans. One-sixth of it is man-made land, built from hillsides cut down and toppled into the sea to form the swollen Shawmut peninsula. Europeans arrived in 1630, and immigrants have left their mark on the streetscape ever since. Low-rise, high-density brick neighborhoods gave way to streetcar suburbs lined with wooden three-deckers, which gave way to the automobile that decimated the city and nearly erased its history.

Boston is my museum, and the buildings within it are the collection. I cycle around the city and photograph items of intrigue to research later. Some items become architectural curiosities that need to be examined more closely, like a Gothic Revival cottage set among a stretching street of three-deckers or a brutalist sculpture plopped like a concrete spaceship in the middle of a neighborhood. To examine something more closely, I paint it, as no one stares more deeply than an artist putting paint on canvas. Here are a few curiosities that led me down a path to better understand what makes Boston, Boston.

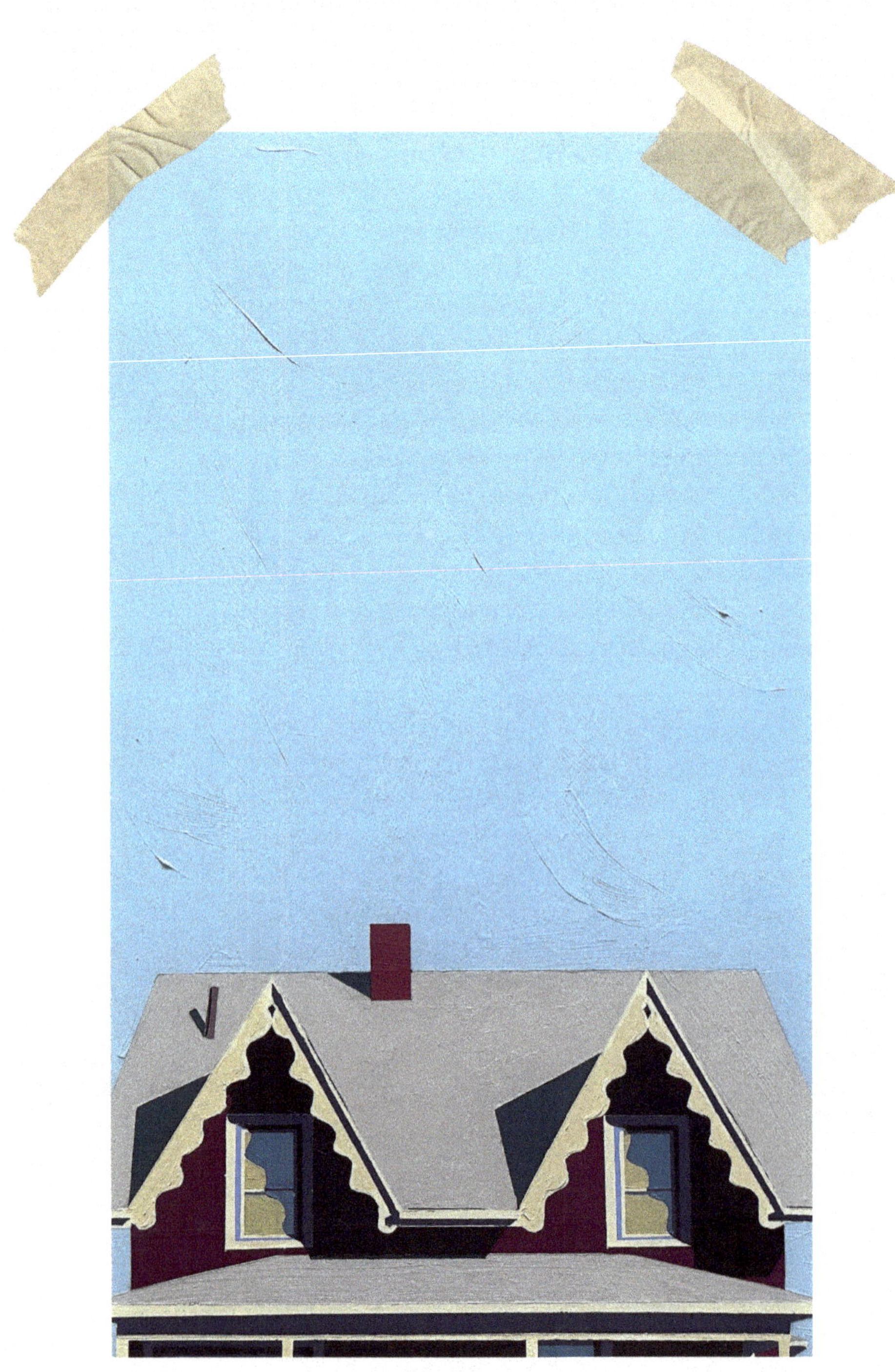

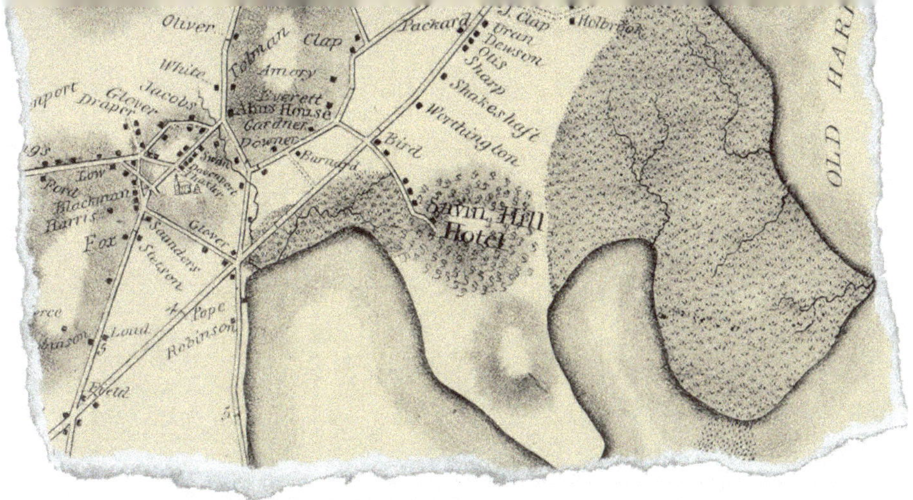

1. The Tuttle House, Dorchester

EYE GOT MY EYES ON YOU. ACRYLIC ON PANEL.

This lovely gothic-style cottage was part of the Tuttle estate. In the late 1800s, it was moved to its present location on Sydney Street from its original location on Savin Hill Ave. Savin Hill Ave, which accessed the Tuttle Estate, is a segment of one of Boston's oldest roads, built in 1630 under a different name, the "Road to Old Hill." But when and why did "Old Hill" become "Savin Hill"? We have Joseph Tuttle to thank for that.

Dorchester was once a very rural area, but the creation of Dorchester Ave in 1804 allowed more Bostonians to access its picturesque shores. Joseph Tuttle (who lived in downtown Boston's Pemberton Square and saw the opportunity to capitalize on Dorchester's growing popularity) purchased an old house in Dorchester and remodeled it into Massachusetts' first seaside hotel, the Tuttle House. It was famous for chicken dinners and winter sleigh parties.

Over time, Tuttle added stables, bowling saloons, and cottages (including the one pictured here) to the property. By 1844, the Old Colony Railroad passed right by the Tuttle estate, and the estate's new visibility called for better branding. In an effort to entice visitors, Tuttle renamed "Old Hill" to "Savin Hill," after the many Savin juniper trees in the area.

The area continued to grow in population, and eventually Dorechester was annexed to Boston. As the city grew denser, it lost its rural seaside vibe. When the Tuttle Estate was eventually sold, the hotel was demolished to make room for a school. But this gothic-style cottage survived!

2. Madison Park High School, Roxbury
THERE ARE INFINITE COLORS FOR CONCRETE. ACRYLIC ON PANEL.

The Madison Park High School in Roxbury was designed in 1968 by Marcel Breuer and completed in 1978, housing some of the most outstanding facilities of any high school of its time. It aimed to be a magnet school, attracting students from all parts of the city into voluntary integrated education. But at what cost?

Madison Park was one of several Boston neighborhoods cleared for "urban renewal." Over 10 acres and hundreds of buildings – including family homes, businesses, health centers, community services, hotels, and churches – were demolished between what is now Melnea Cass Boulevard and Malcolm X Boulevard. Melnea Cass is itself an urban scar, a vestige of an abandoned urban highway project called the Inner Belt.

In an effort to stop the destruction of their neighborhoods, residents of Jamaica Plain, Roxbury, the South End, and Cambridge all rallied together to form a group called People Before Highways. Theirs is one of only a few successful examples of a group that stood up against the federal government and won. The highway was never built, but neighborhood scars still remain.

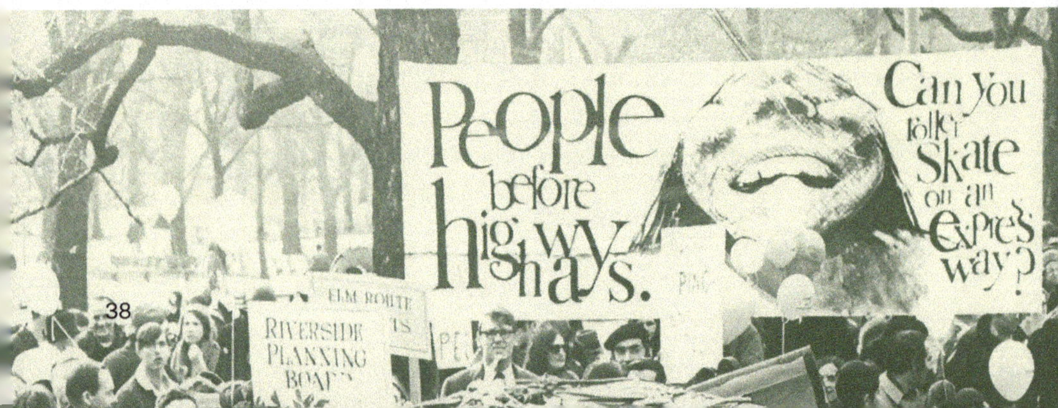

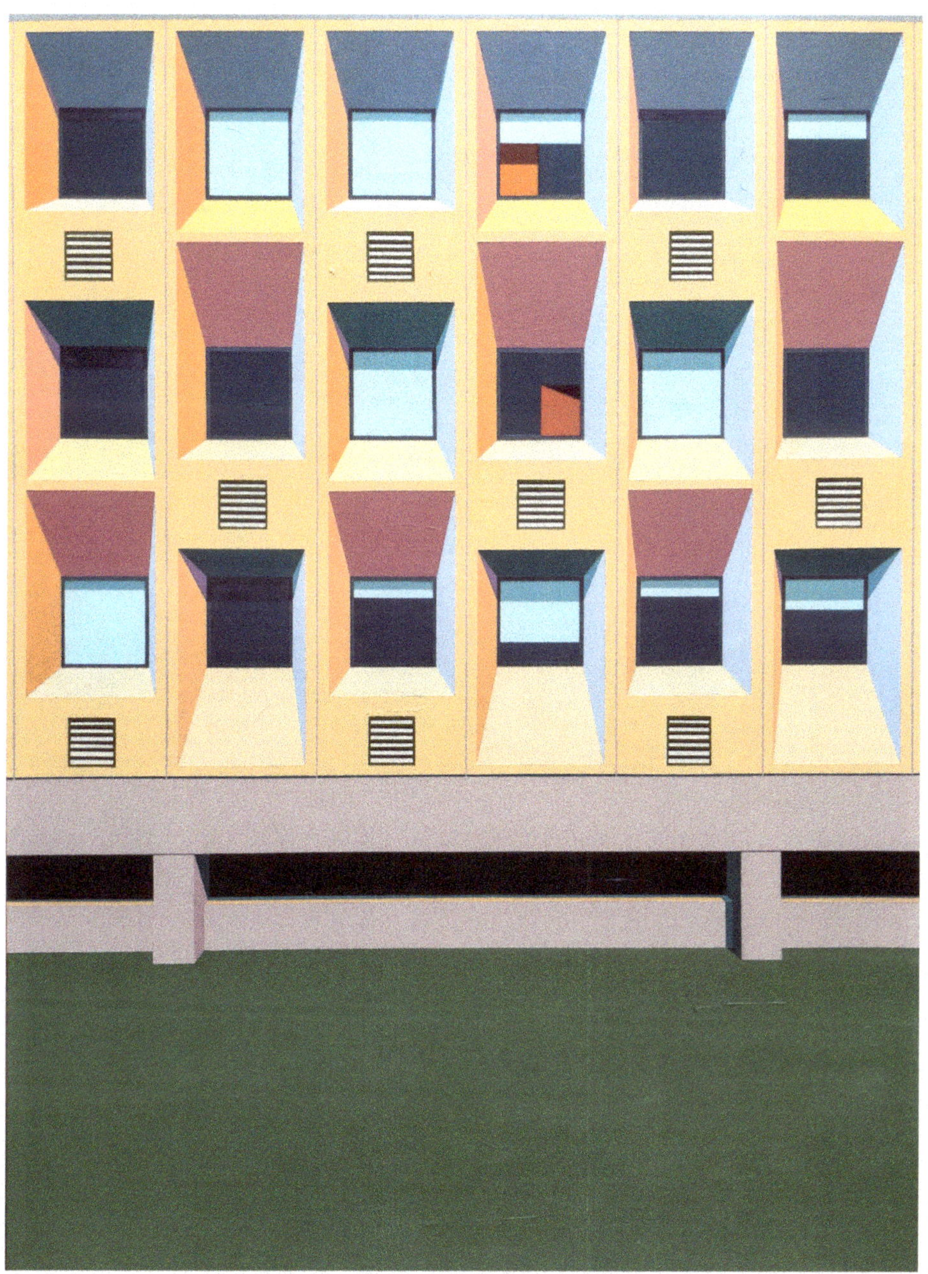

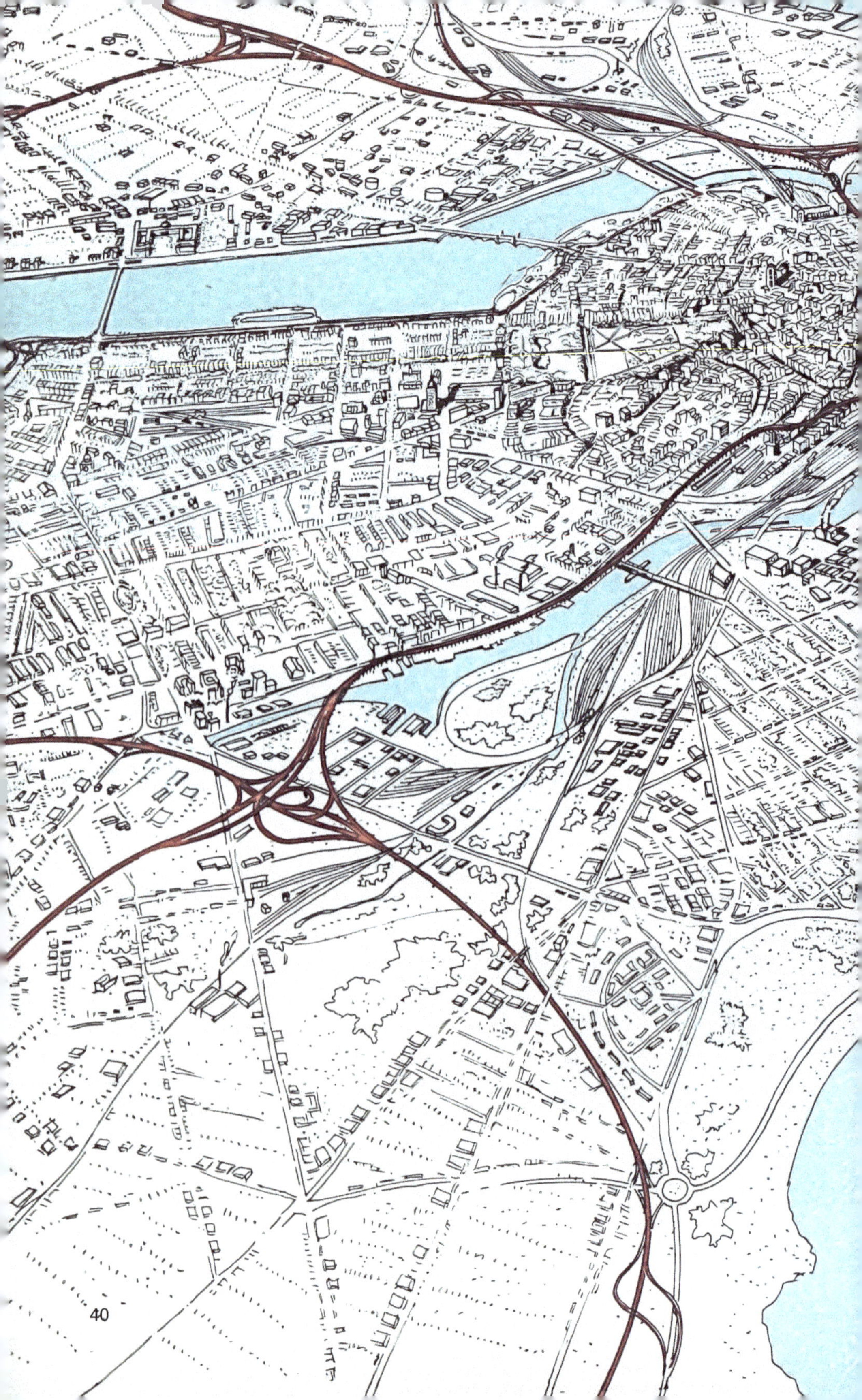

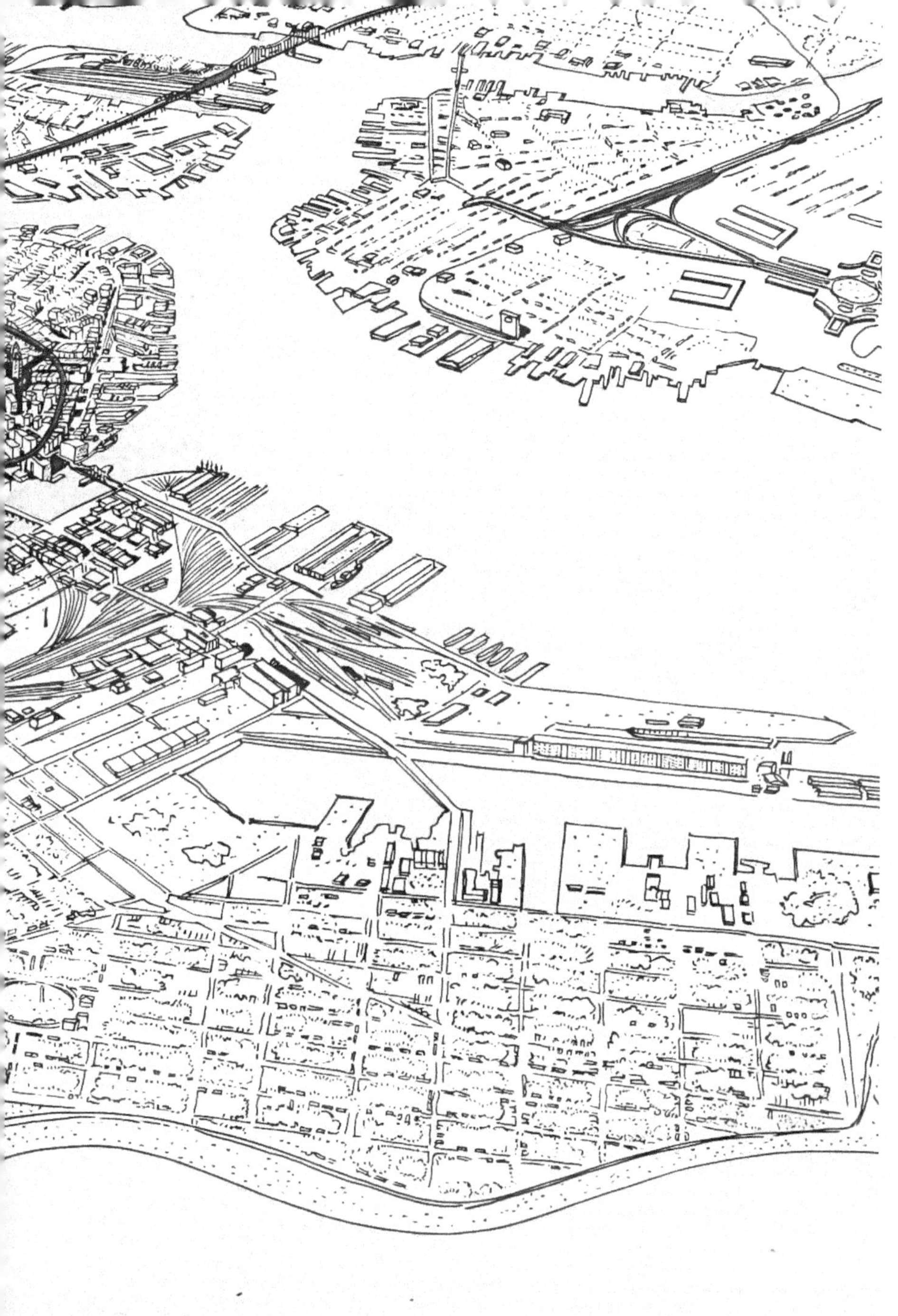

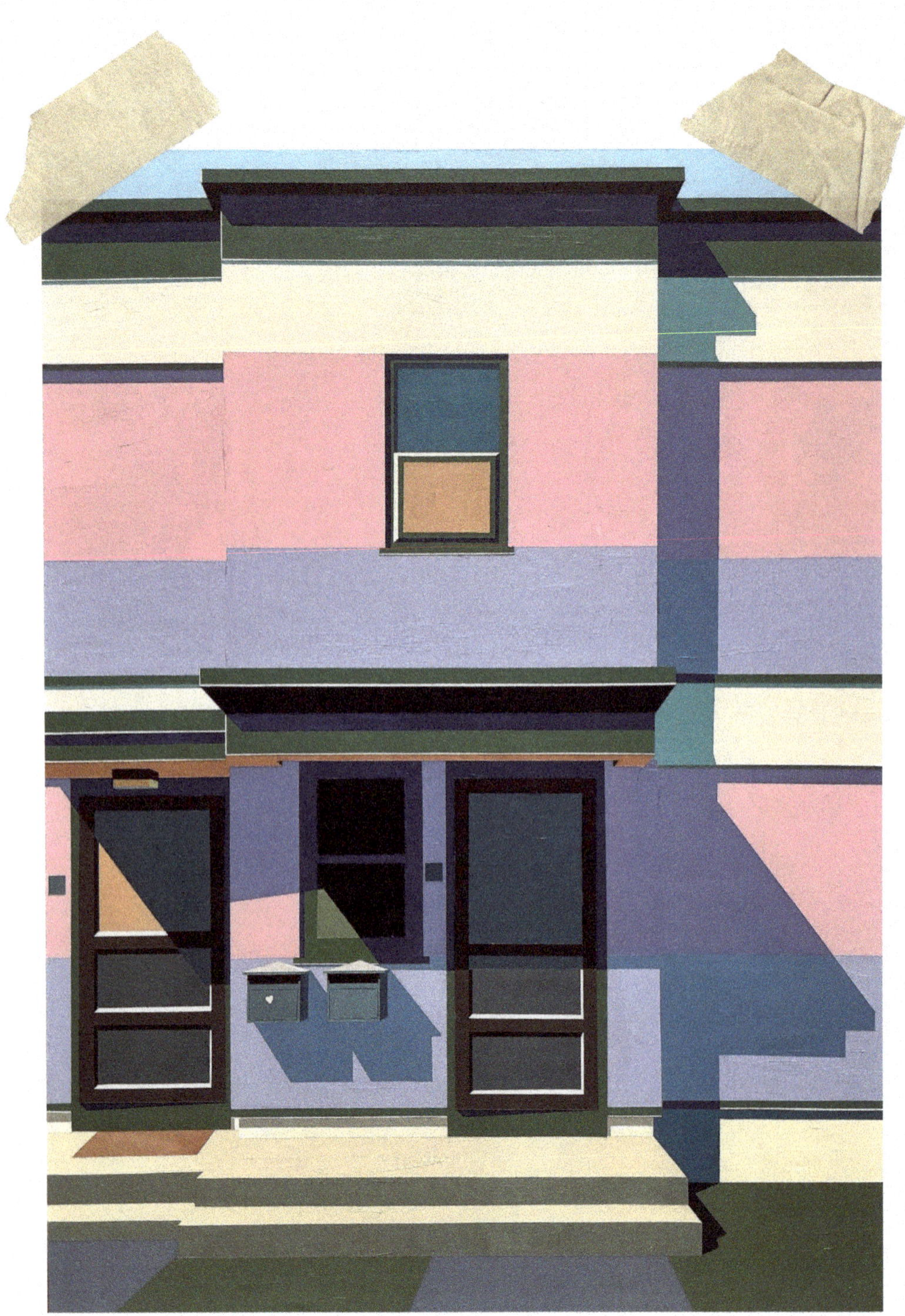

3. Frederick Douglass Historic District, Lower Roxbury

You won't find the Frederick Douglass Historic District in a guidebook or a history textbook. The district narrowly missed erasure, and without People Before Highways, it wouldn't exist at all.

The area was one of the last parcels of man-made land to be developed in Boston. The land was largely owned by Robert Treat Paine, who purchased it from the Tremont Development Company in the 1880s in order to build small-scale affordable housing "for the working man." The diminutive buildings that fill the streetscape are human-scaled and visually entertaining, with decorative brickwork and architectural bays that break up the space, unlike the contemporary trend of glass walls.

These well designed and affordable homes became popular residences for Black families moving north during the Great Migration; many men in the neighborhood worked for the train lines as Pullman Porters.

When White Flight struck (and suburbanites wanted easy access to the city via automobile), large swaths of land were demolished to clear room for highways under the pretense of "urban renewal." At one point, Frederick Douglass Historic District was next on the chopping block, but People Before Highways saved the neighborhood from becoming a highway.

This newer row of affordable housing was built in the 1970s, filling in the scar of the abandoned highway project. It mimics the affordable housing across the street, built 100 years earlier.

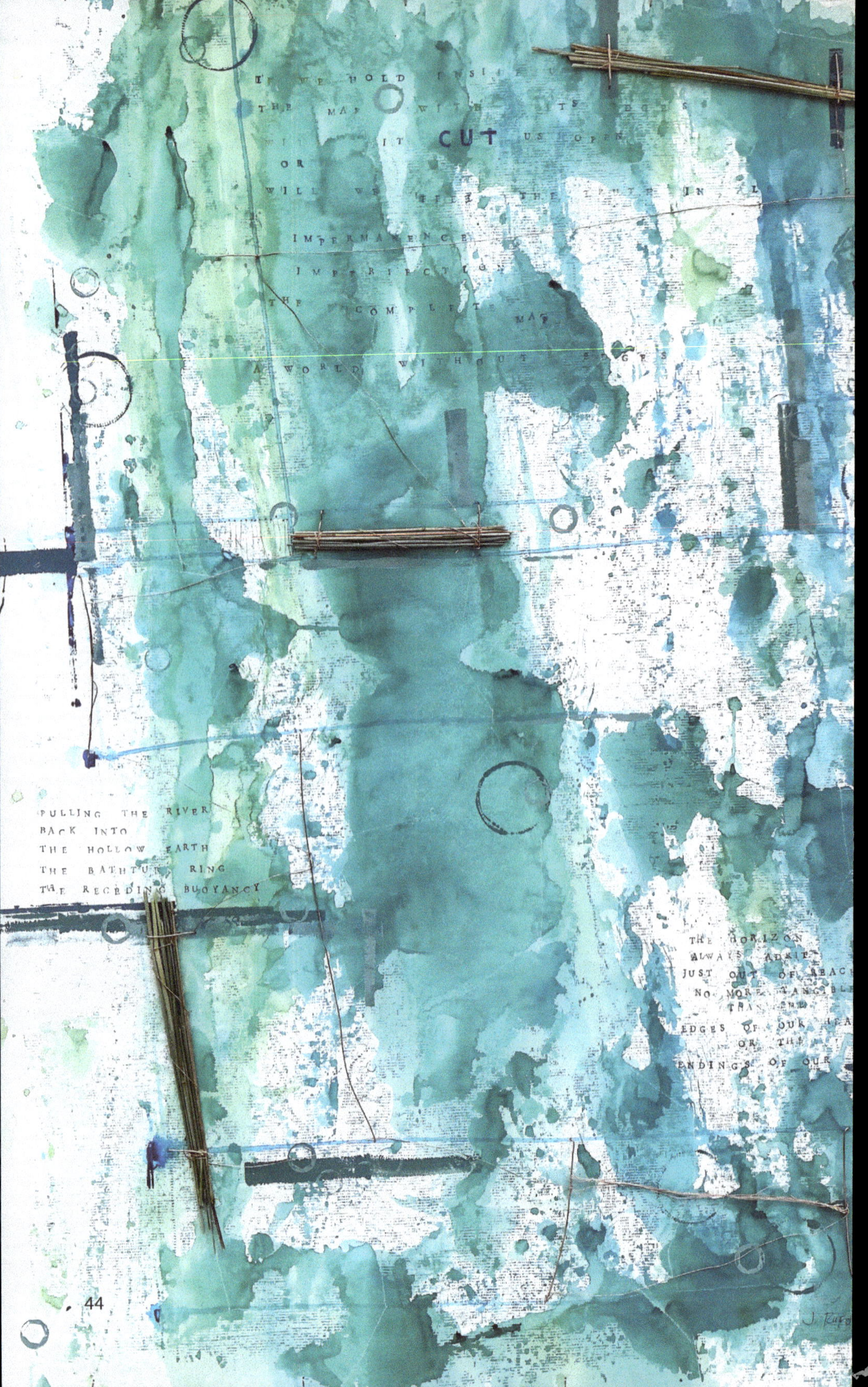

44

Without Edges,
painting and poem

John Rufo

If we hold inside us
The map with it's edges
Will it cut us open

Or

Will we see the truth in all things
Impermanence
Imperfection
The incomplete map
A world without edges

Pulling the river
Back into
The hollow earth
The bathtub ring
The receding buoyancy

The horizon
Always adrift
Just out of reach
No more tangible
Than the
Edges of our hearts
Or the
Endings of our deeds

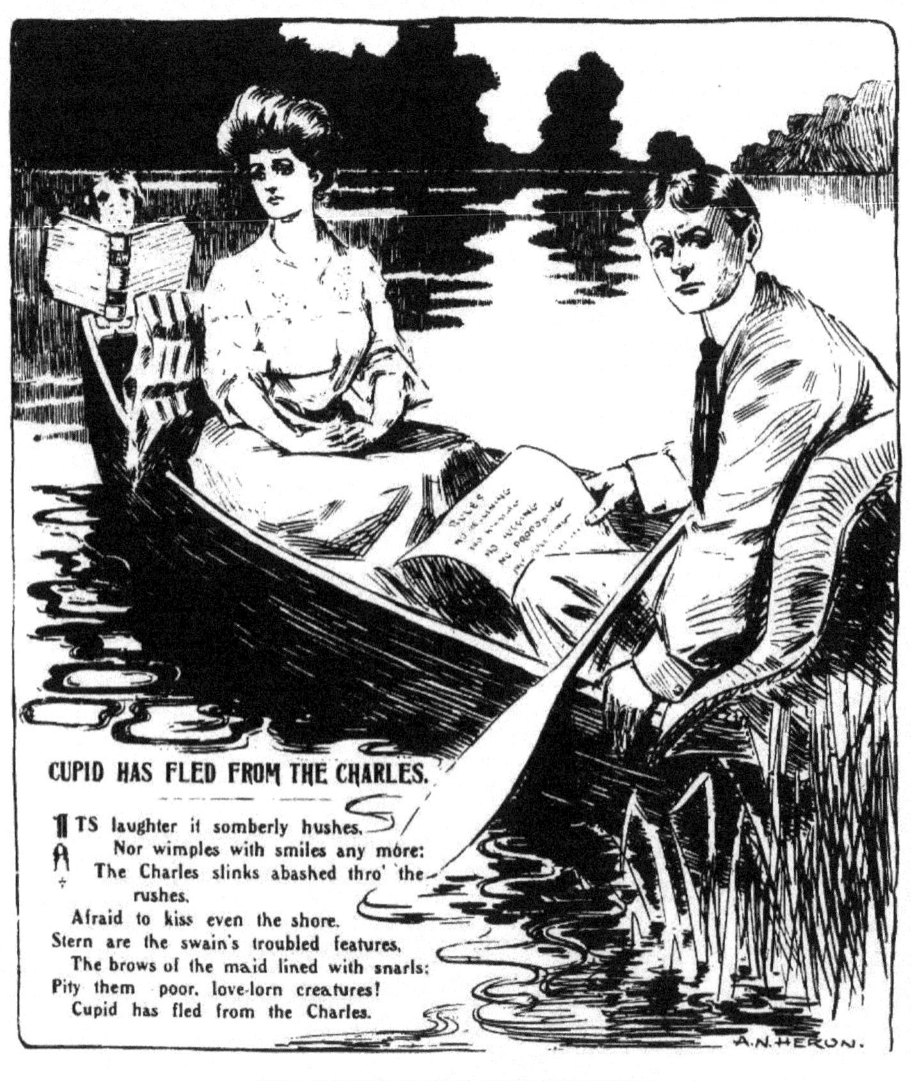

NOW THERE'S GLOOM UPON THE RIVER.

1903 — ARTIST REACTS TO BOSTON'S CANOODLING CRACK DOWN IN RESPONSE TO COMPLAINTS ABOUT "OBSCENE AND INDECENT ACTS" TAKING PLACE ON THE CHARLES RIVER. THE "SIT UP STRAIGHT OR FACE ARREST" CAMPAIGN CHARGED ANYONE LYING DOWN IN A CANOE WITH A $20 FINE.

CONTRIBUTOR BIOS

ABBEY CAHILL IS A BOSTON-BASED WRITER AND THE FOUNDER OF THE Q. SHE IS INTERESTED IN THE RELATIONSHIP BETWEEN WHERE WE LIVE AND WHO WE ARE.

ERWIN KAMUENE IS A CONGOLESE-AMERICAN BOSTON-BASED WRITER DEDICATED TO USING THE FORM AS A MEANS OF REVEALING HIMSELF AND THE WORLD AROUND HIM. WHEN HE'S NOT READING OR WRITING OR PROCRASTINATING DOING ONE OR THE OTHER, HE CAN USUALLY BE FOUND COOKING HIS FAVORITE RECIPES AND/OR WATCHING HIS FAVORITE MOVIES.

GOLDEN IS A BLACK GENDER-NONCONFORMING TRANS PHOTOGRAPHER, POET, & COMMUNITY ORGANIZER. THEY ARE THE AUTHOR OF <u>ON LEARNING HOW TO LIVE</u>, A PHOTOGRAPHIC SERIES DOCUMENTING BLACK TRANS LIFE AT THE INTERSECTIONS OF SURVIVING & LIVING IN THE UNITED STATES. AMONG MANY OTHER FELLOWSHIPS, GOLDEN HAS BEEN A RECIPIENT OF THE ISABELLA STEWART GARDNER MUSEUM LUMINARIES FELLOWSHIP (2019) AND THE CITY OF BOSTON ARTIST-IN-RESIDENCE (2020-2021). SEE MORE OF THEIR WORK AT GOLDENGOLDENGOLDEN.COM.

JOHN RUFO IS AN ARCHITECT AND ARTIST LIVING IN PRACTICING IN NEEDHAM MASSACHUSETTS. JOHN ATTENDED THE RHODE ISLAND SCHOOL OF DESIGN WHERE HE MAJORED IN ARCHITECTURE AND FELL IN LOVE WITH THE DRAWING PROCESS AS A FORM OF SELF-INQUIRY. JOHN'S INTERESTS AND PURSUITS RANGE FROM DRAWING & PAINTING TO CLASSICAL CHINESE AND JAPANESE POETRY, BIRD-WATCHING AND FAMILY TIME WITH HIS WIFE AND TWO DAUGHTERS.

LINDA CABOT IS AN ARTIST, POET, AND COMMUNITY PHILANTHROPIST WITH DEEP NEW ENGLAND ROOTS, WORKING AT THE INTERSECTION OF ART AND ENVIRONMENTAL EDUCATION. SHE IS THE FOUNDER OF BOW SEAT OCEAN AWARENESS PROGRAMS AND A TRUSTEE OF THE NEW ENGLAND AQUARIUM AND THE ISABELLA STUART GARDNER MUSEUM,

MATTHEW DICKEY IS A PAINTER, PHOTOGRAPHER, AND LOCAL TOUR GUIDE LIVING IN DORCHESTER. AS A "STREETSCAPE CURATOR" HE HOPES TO SHARE CONTEXT ABOUT WHY CITIES LOOK THE WAY THEY DO. SEE MORE OF HIS WORK OR BOOK A TOUR AT MATTHEWADICKEY.COM.

MILES HOWARD IS A JOURNALIST AND URBAN TRAIL BUILDER PASSIONATE ABOUT OUTDOOR RECREATION, WALKABLE ENVIRONMENTS, AND THE QUESTION OF WHO HAS ACCESS TO THESE SPACES. HIS WRITING OFTEN SPOTLIGHTS THE ACTIVISTS, CREATORS, AND POLICY MAKERS WHO ARE WORKING TO MAKE URBAN RECREATION MORE INVITING AND INCLUSIVE. SEE MORE OF HIS WORK AT MILESHOWARD.COM.

SAM LINBERG GREW UP IN WEST ROXBURY WITH HIS DAD, MOM, SISTER, TWO DOGS, AND CAT. HE IS A CURRENT STUDENT AT NOBLE AND GREENOUGH SCHOOL, WHERE HE RECENTLY HAD THE OPPORTUNITY TO EXPLORE HIS HOMETOWN THROUGH AN AP PHOTOGRAPHY CLASS.

TAHIRA MUHAMMAD, A SENIOR AT THE NOBLE AND GREENOUGH SCHOOL, IS FROM HYDE PARK IN BOSTON, MA. SHE WILL ATTEND DARTMOUTH COLLEGE THIS FALL AND PLAY FOR THEIR BASKETBALL TEAM. CURIOUS AND PASSIONATE, TAHIRA EXPRESSES HER CREATIVITY AND STORYTELLING THROUGH PHOTOGRAPHY.